Real Estate
Money Machine

REAL ESTATE MONEY MACHINE

*An Investment
Guide for
the Nineties*

A REVISED EDITION

WADE B. COOK

Lighthouse Publishing Group, Inc.
Distributed by Midpoint Trade Books, Inc.

"This publication is designed to provide accurate and authoritative
information in regard to the subject matter covered. It is sold with the
understanding that the publisher is not engaged in rendering legal,
accounting, or other professional service. If legal or other expert
assistance is required, the services of a competent professional person
should be sought."
From a declaration of principles
jointly adopted by a committee of the American Bar Association
and committee of the Publishers Association

ISBN: 0-910019-62-2

Published in the United States by:
The Lighthouse Publishing Group
an imprint of
U.S.A., Inc.,
a subsidiary of Profit Financial Corporation.
Ticker symbol PFNL
24837 104th Ave. SE, Suite 201
Kent, WA 98031

Distributed by Kampmann & Co., New York

Printed in the U.S.A.   Fourth Edition
10 9 8 7 6 5 4 3 2

This new and revised edition

is dedicated to my wife, Laura,

our girls Brenda, Carrie, Leslie,

and Rachel, and our son Benjamin:

a family that is a new and wonderful

revision to my life.

Contents

Preface

Would you like to have a million dollars, or would you rather have what a million dollars could do for you? Several years ago my economics professor asked this question. He told us that a million dollars would earn $167 a day in the bank. "I could live on that," he joked, "if I didn't eat so much." We all talked about having the million dollars, but out of our discussions came the conclusion that, even though having the money would be nice, having the income created by the million dollars would be even nicer.

A while ago, my publisher was giving me some advice. "We have enough books on how to make a million dollars. Can you write a book on how to make a living?" I'm taking his challenge. This book is a guideline for building a monthly income. The equities will be there, but you can LIVE on the monthly payments if needed while payments keep coming in.

I present here an investment idea for the nineties that could increase your income and net worth if you're an investor, or help create an income and net worth if you're a novice. The reason I use the word IDEA is because this is not a "magic, get-rich-quick formula." It is a sensible, attainable approach – with new answers to old questions.

There was a time I needed new answers – lots of new answers – because the old formulas weren't working for me.

My story then was like that of many investors. When I was in my early twenties and a little disenchanted with middle income America, I went in search of something – a formula to get ahead. The time was the early seventies and all the talk centered on real estate. I picked up a few of the books popular at that time and started reading. The theories seemed good and I was excited to get started, but I didn't have any money. It wasn't until a few years later that the opportunity came.

I lived two doors down from a small house that went up for sale. It was a cute little place and I thought it would make the "perfect rental." After a few bargaining sessions with the owner, the house was mine. I spent a few days cleaning and painting, and by the weekend it was rented. It seemed almost too easy to be true. That adventure whetted my investing appetite, so I dug out the old books and read them again. At that time, when the economy was good and interest rates were lower, these books seemed to offer some realistic advice.

I kept my eyes open for other houses and, sure enough, doors opened. I looked at many, bought a few, and then realized that I had become an investor through and through. About one year after my first investment I was making enough money in real estate to quit my job and become a full-time investor. It was exciting to devote my time to looking at houses, talking with real estate agents and calling on homesellers. Never before had I had such control of my time.

Everything was going well until one day some bills came due and I didn't have the money to pay them. This was upsetting to me, but more so to my wife (as most of you self-employed people can verify). How could this happen? I had EQUITIES! I soon realized that ownership doesn't mean cash flow – that having assets is not synonymous with having money in your pocket. I didn't realize when I went on my own that most of what I did was going to be controlled by someone else.

During this period I experienced time problems that almost drove me crazy: a seller who was out of town and tying up my money, so I was not able to make other offers; the escrow company that was waiting for something to come in the mail; the bank that wouldn't send the assumption papers; the attorney who looked over the final papers and wanted to make several changes. Months would go by and all my energies would be exhausted just trying to get one deal closed. These delays took some of the excitement out of investing because I was controlled by someone else – working within their time frame, meeting their requirements, etc. *FHA requirements take to long*

One day I was about to sign another earnest money agreement to sell a house FHA. I didn't have much cash and I was looking at two problems: the additional cash I would need to fix up the house to meet FHA requirements, and the extremely long time it would take to close and receive my money. I asked myself, "Wouldn't it be better to sell on contract? (For a definition of the word *contract*, please see the end of this preface.) Couldn't I make more money in the long run if I could close sooner and reinvest the down payment in one or two more places?" I knew I could close the house on contract by that Friday. All day I penciled out this idea on paper and could hardly believe the figures.

Quick Profits and Big Equities

Had I sold the house FHA it would have taken about five months to receive my $12,000 profit. My figures showed that, in the same time period, I could take a $4,000 down payment and turn it into $150,000 in equities with about $1,200 a month net coming in on my net monthly payments. I put it to the test and the results surprised me (even though I had written it down five months earlier). My actual equities were $151,000 and my net monthly payments were $1,290. As I continued to invest using this approach, it got even better.

When friends and other investors asked me about these ideas, I began giving seminars – in my home and office, at the community college, and at real estate offices. This investment idea soon caught on and seemed to work for anyone who tried it – anyone, that is, who didn't live to cash out. It was a way for novice or experienced investors to have cash flow in the present, equity growth for the future, and tax advantages for both time frames, all at a rate faster than they thought possible.

The economic climate is now slower and tight money makes it necessary to change the nature of investing. Many of the old formulas don't apply; and while everyone is waiting for a new game plan, the institutions with the money just continue to say no. Buying and selling isn't what it used to be. Everyone is sitting on the sidelines waiting for something to break.

NOW is the time the information in this book is really needed. The theory is sound. The rate of equity growth will astound you, and the tax advantages of selling on installments will pleasantly surprise you. There is obviously a great need for new ideas in the real estate market today, and that's exactly what I have to offer. What's more important is that the ideas in this book will stimulate your mind—creating even more ideas for your particular situation.

The contents of this book can help any investor. However, if you think you're past the stage of the average small investor, I suggest that you glance at the first few chapters (Chapter 8 is a must), then skip to the last chapter which is written for the investor with some excess cash flow.

I tested this investment hypothesis and it worked. Now let it work for you and in just a few years you could have what a million dollars would do for you. The ideas presented here are easy to understand and just as easy to implement. By reading this book you can learn how to build your own *Real Estate Money Machine!*

CONTRACT: A DEFINITION

Throughout the book I use the word contract. My own definition of contract is any type of owner financing. It is an agreement for purchasing or selling real property. You may use a <u>Uniform Real Estate Contract</u>, a <u>Land Mortgage</u>, or as is becoming popular now, an AITD or <u>All Inclusive Trust Deed</u>. When I buy, I give the seller a Mortgage or Trust Deed for the equity. This Deed of Trust (or Trust Deed in some states) or Mortgage is accompanied by a note which states the terms.

[handwritten: can use!]

[handwritten: 1) Uniform Real Estate Contract]

Publisher's Note

[handwritten: 2) land Mortgage]

[handwritten: 3) AITD]

Mr. Cook has authored a new book entitled *The First National Bank of Real Estate Clauses* with over a thousand clauses and phrases for effectively buying and selling property. There is one <u>phrase, an exculpatory clause</u>, which will help assure that the only collateral for the note is the real property and does not extend to your other assets. This one phrase alone would make the purchase of this book worthwhile. Look in the back for information on how to order this and other books.

[handwritten: Siang: what is An "Exculpatory clause"]

The Problem

Before this investment idea can be fully appreciated, one must understand the questions it answers, the problems it solves, and the headaches it avoids.

In my first twelve months of investing, I was able to purchase nine houses and not one of these transactions was handled in the same way. Each was unique, but I managed to get them all sold or rented. My investing really picked up and I thought I had found my niche in life, so I quit my job. About this time, something happened to my plans: I was losing control of my cash flow.

The investment books I'd read were written from the sole premise of buying and fixing up in order to eventually cash out and reinvest in larger units. I must admit I made money, but in most instances cashing out created several problems: I had too much money buried in each property for too long, and the time factor in waiting for the cash-out caused a fleet of hardships. Also, on April 15, Uncle Sam was going to be waiting with a noose because of all the cash I'd received at once. In order to save my neck I decided to change my tactics.

I searched for information to make my investing more effective. I spent countless hours reading and posing questions to professionals who knew about real estate. There were plenty of people who knew bits and pieces of the investment game, but very few had comprehensive knowledge that could be depended on for all types of real estate transactions. It became obvious I was getting only pat answers because other people were all investing with the same investment formulas. It took a year of dealing with these problems before I asked myself the question, "Isn't there an easier, more profitable way?" The answer to that question didn't come overnight. As you read the following examples of the problems I experienced, you'll understand why I decided it was time for a new approach. In chapter two you'll read how I solved these problems.

Problem #1: Government Financing—FHA/VA

"I think I've just sold your house. May I come over and present this offer to you?"

Sound familiar? I hadn't had the house on the market very long and already offers were coming in. When Sue from Bingo Realty arrived and laid the earnest money agreement down in front of me, I was surprised because it was for the exact amount I was asking ($50,000). She said the people were extremely qualified and they'd breeze through the buyer qualification the VA requires for loan approval. This was too good to be true; I was getting exactly what I asked for. (Wow! I just didn't know what I was asking for!) What happened over the next several months seemed like a mini-nightmare.

"First of all, they'll have to qualify."

"Who takes care of that?"

"I do. As a matter of fact, I'll take care of everything." Then she walked out the door with the next four months of my life in her briefcase.

Instead of two weeks to qualify, it took four. Part of their income wouldn't count because he was self-employed part-time and didn't keep the best records. But, after a few adjustments here and there, they finally qualified.

About this time the inspection report came in on the house. I wasn't worried that it was five pages long. What hurt was they didn't even double space when listing all the things that needed repairing, and the list still filled up every available space on the inspection sheet. I figured the additional work would cost close to $2,000 and take an extra month. It did. Two house payments later, I had my second appointment with the VA House Inspector. I was about five minutes late. One word of advice—don't be late. Hell hath no fury like an inspector scorned. It took fifteen minutes before we were talking. Actually, I was talking the whole fifteen minutes trying to get him to smile. He took a few notes and left.

About two weeks later his reinspection report came in saying to remove a little dirt touching one of the basement window sills. I drove over and kicked the dirt away with my shoe. The inspector probably spent more time writing the report than it would have taken him to do it himself. (It seems they either like you or they don't.) Another house payment came due.

After this, I finally thought I was getting somewhere. The buyers were anxious to move in and I was anxious to get my money. I thought everyone was on the same team. How uninformed I was. There was one other party in this transaction who hadn't played a big part until now. You guessed it—the banker. Apparently, this banker felt he could act in his own "best interest." Pardon the pun, but interest is the name of the game. Frankly put, points are the amount the bank is going to charge the seller for making the loan.

Why is the seller charged? After all, it isn't his idea to get the loan or use the bank. Why does he have to pay? VA to the BUYER'S rescue. There is a rule which states the buyer can only be charged so much for loan fees, and because the FHA/ VA dictate how much interest the participating banks can charge, the banks have devised a system to collect—up front —what they figure they'll lose over the course of the loan. What frustrates me is, if the house is resold at any time before the loan is paid off, no points are ever returned to the seller and they are charged AGAIN to the new seller at the new selling price. These loans are guaranteed by the FHA/VA, which means, in case of foreclosure the government would pick up the tab—paying off the house. See how the banks watch out for their own interest? Have I made my point?

The points at the time I signed this particular earnest money agreement were one and a half—meaning 1 1/2 percent of the selling price, or $750, would be paid to the bank by me. The interest rate the buyer was to pay was 9 1/2 percent.

I was told several times by one of the escrow officers that everything was ready to close, so I couldn't understand the continued delay that dragged on over a month. I was tired of their excuses, but it was "supposed to close any day now." It was two weeks before Christmas and, if it hadn't been for my family being so happy in spite of the bank, Christmas would have been bleak indeed.

About mid-January, the phone rang. "You can come in and sign the papers now," said the escrow officer. Inside of two minutes I was in the car heading out to pick up my money.

"Why is this amount $2,000 less than what I planned on?" I asked, expecting an apology for the error. The answer was on the closing statement which was pushed in front of my face. Closing statements are usually fun, but this one had some strange figures on it. During the time it took to close, the points rose to SIX, which doesn't sound bad until you realize the other 4 1/2 percent added another $2,250 to my costs. There was also a Warehouse Interest Adjustment Fee which I'll talk about in the next section as well as a few other costs.

The buyers' costs were not affected by this, although the interest rate on their loan had gone up to 10 percent because the original agreement had passed the interest rate commitment date. Decision time. Do I go through with it or do I back out? That was no easy decision. I knew if I backed out now, I'd probably be sued for performance. (This means I'd probably be forced legally to go through with the deal. Meanwhile, I'd still be making the monthly payments.) It was ready to close now and I desperately needed the money. The decision was made.

I signed the papers and stood there waiting for the check. "Not now," said the girl. "The papers have to be recorded and it's too late for that today. We'll record tomorrow and you can pick up the check Monday." I was rather upset with this whole set of affairs and upon leaving I looked the loan officer in the eyes and said, "I know you've been postponing this until the points went up." Silence. He looked at me and smiled.

Monday—I thought I could finally make offers on two other houses that I thought I had lost because this deal had taken so long for me to get my money. I drove out to pick up the check only to be told that it was "in the mail." It arrived Thursday.

This was such a raw deal that I started asking myself some important questions. There had to be better ways of doing the same thing. I was determined to get back in control and find those ways, or create them.

Benefits

In spite of the problems they cause, I feel there's a place and a time for government lending agencies; FHA and VA financing plans are too important to the home owner just to dismiss them because they're cumbersome. The FHA and VA not only set up rules for the banks and mortgage companies, they also dictate loan approval requirements for the buyers and the properties. This can be a big problem. From remodeling an "old beater" to new construction they are there with their mountains of regulations and paperwork. For the private homeowner much of this is to his advantage. If I didn't know the contractor and the quality of his work I, too, would much rather live in an FHA/VA approved home knowing the house at least met some standards.

Many of the buyers out there can only purchase a home under FHA or VA terms. These plans offer low down payments and lower interest rates, keeping the monthly payments down. They also stipulate foreclosure provisions which are weighted in favor of the buyer.

However, because so many buyers want these benefits, the loan demand has put a heavy burden on the FHA/VA, causing delays in processing time. These regulations can create several other problems, which invariably involve money—your money if you are the seller. If the house you're selling needs repairs, you must understand the regulations, follow the written requirements, search for the proper materials, and make sure that whoever is doing the work does it right. Complying with these regulations can cost dearly. It also creates a time problem, adding to the misery created by FHA/VA in-house delays. Remember the monthly payments; I know everyone would like to forget them, but they march on. My longest closing took about six months, and with payments of $540 per month (totaling $3,240) it's a good way to wipe out any cash flow you have coming from other sources.

If you can overlook the problems of regulations and time delays (which you can only afford to do if you're the buyer), there are some FHA/VA benefits for the small investor. Most of their loans are readily assumable by anyone, even corporations. It means taking over payments with interest rates far below what you would be paying the bank or the current seller.

For example, I made an offer on a house which included the assumption of an older FHA loan. The agent told me it was about 7 1/2 percent so I was excited. When I arrived back at his office I was told it looked more like 6 1/2 percent and my excitement grew. About a week later I was talking to the seller and I mentioned the 6 1/2 percent. He said, "Oh, no. I think it's 5 3/4 percent." When I heard that, I called the escrow company. They said the assumption figures had just arrived from the bank. I was really anxious for them to verify the 5 3/4 percent. "Ahhh, it's not quite that; he lied to you. It's 5 1/4 percent." I wanted to hear that again! I wanted to hear it several times again. I was so excited I could hardly drive.

Maybe it's crazy to get excited over assuming $4,400 at 5 1/4 percent, but there are certain things investors are allowed to get excited about—assuming low interest rates is one of them. We had a celebration party.

The next benefit of FHA/VA loans will be best understood by investors who consider themselves builders. Construction financing is almost always short term (approximately six months) and the interest rates are a healthy cut above regular mortgage rates, so the builder needs to cash out. Because so many buyers want FHA/VA benefits, the builders need to sell that way or many of them would be out of business. Usually, all excess interest costs and the time factor for selling FHA/VA are taken into account at the beginning. For persons absolutely needing to cash out (assuming they have the time and money to wait) this is one way to go.

Last Benefit

The last benefit is based on more than just figures or time. It's partly because of FHA/VA programs that America has become a nation of homeowners. Put whatever value you want on that (there are several), but to me as an investor, it means there are a lot of people who want a piece of the rock. Their desire to own their own home is strong, but in today's economy that desire can't always be met, so there needs to be a new approach.

FHA/VA financing has given a chunk of owning America to many Americans. Originally, government financing came along at a time of great distress in our economy. Banks were afraid to loan money and most people couldn't qualify anyway. The federal government entered with good intentions and a lot of other people's tax money; after all, they wouldn't actually be loaning the money, they would just guarantee the loans. Now, the banks and mortgage companies had nothing to lose but a little interest. But, with a little creativity (like adding a few additional charges, i.e., points), they were also able to eliminate this deficiency and lose nothing.

Be smart. Use these plans to your best advantage. Stay one step ahead by being educated—knowing what these plans will or won't do for you.

Problem #3: Conventional Financing

Conventional financing simply means someone goes to the bank to get a loan to buy a house. The problems here are nothing like government insured loans, but there are some things to be aware of.

Once again, the first consideration is money—your money. The bank stays in complete control, sometimes to their disadvantage. The following story is so incredible that even I find it hard to believe.

I made an earnest money offer on a house my wife and I wanted to live in. It was a beautiful brick home in a nice neighborhood. My offer was very close to the asking price; the owner wanted $120,000 and I offered $110,000. This was accepted so I went to a savings and loan to borrow the money. We spent several hours filling out all their forms and then they ordered an appraisal of the property.

Within a couple of weeks the bank said the loan was not approved. I couldn't understand why because everything had seemed so right. I was informed that the computer kicked it out because it didn't fit their formulas. I inquired further and found out that the property had appraised at $160,000. According to their formula the selling price couldn't deviate more than 20 percent from the appraised value.

Now, no reasonable person would refuse a loan with EXTRA collateral, if all the other conditions were met. Apparently, though, this company was not reasonable. I really wanted the house, but only on my terms. We argued back and forth for about three weeks, but because the strain was getting to be too much I just dropped it. I wanted to take their computer and dump it in the ocean with an epitaph on it reading, "May you *rust* in peace."

Now all savings and loan companies are not this bad; nevertheless, they do want to keep control. For instance, suppose the appraisal comes in lower than the selling price you and the buyer have agreed on. The loan would be adjusted and you would receive the lower amount.

Suppose your buyer qualifies for a loan but the bank will not guarantee the interest rate. Four weeks later, when it's ready to close, the interest rate has increased, which, in turn, increases the house payment. Now, because his "income to payments" ratio doesn't fit their formula, your buyer no longer qualifies. The deal is off and you are out looking for a new buyer. Guess who gets to make all the house payments in the meantime?

On another deal, I was sitting in the bank getting ready to sign the closing papersand going over the closing statement when I noticed an extra charge for $80 with the title, "Warehouse Interest Adjustment Fee." (Have you ever seen a bank's warehouse? Neither have I!) That meant $80 less to me, so I questioned the agent. She said I'd have to take it up with her supervisor. When he came in, he explained that the charge was there because they were having to borrow money at a higher rate than when they started processing this loan.

I said, "Listen, I'm the SELLER here. I didn't come in for this loan—my buyers did. Why are you charging me loan fees?" He said, "Well, we can only charge the buyers so much and we need more to pay for the higher costs of our money." I said, "I don't care what you have to pay for your money. The buyer is borrowing the money from you to get into my house. We had an agreement in writing and I don't want to pay this $80." His response: "We are doing it to everyone."

I said, "Gary, let's suppose one day your employees go to lunch and while they're gone you take $80 out of their purses. When they come back they notice that their money is missing and they say, 'Gary, what's going on here?' You answer, 'We're running a business here, but we're just not making enough money. Sorry, I just had to take it. I had to take a little bit from all of you so we can keep the business going.'"

Gary just looked at me and smiled.

Then I said, "Gary, let's bring it to you a little more personally. Let's say Friday you get your paycheck and there's an extra $80 deducted. You're a little upset about this so you call the payroll officer and say, 'Hey! Why has this $80 been taken out of my paycheck?' And she says, 'Look, Gary, we know you're a nice guy and a good employee, but we're having to pay a little bit more for our money than we'd planned on. Business costs are going up, but hey, don't worry. Gary, we're doing it to everybody.'"

Tired of my logic, he gave me two choices: Sign the papers or back out of the deal. I was looking at a $13,000 check coming to me and I really didn't want to back out. So, I signed the papers under protest, adding the note:

"I do not agree with this charge. If it is withheld from my proceeds it is against my best interest and against my will."

I thought, possibly I could go back and sue them, not realizing at the time how naive I was. They were the largest bank in the state and it probably would have cost me ten times that amount to take them to court. So I signed the papers and took my money and, again, learned a lesson: Investors should not do business with banks.

The banks want to control everything: the selling price (they usually have their own appraisers); the necessary down payment (controlling who can or cannot buy); interest rates (which tend to fluctuate upwards during the processing time of the loan); closing time (the faster you want it to close, the longer they take); the length of time the loan will run (this amortization time determines the monthly payment amount, so again the bank controls who qualifies and who doesn't); and prepayment penalties on the loan if the buyer decides to pay it off early. If you would really like to see more of the controls they take, read over their security agreements the buyer must sign.

Another thing, if you want to buy or sell a house with an existing bank loan, they can raise the interest rate at the time of sale (which would then raise the monthly payments) or call the loan due (so they can get their money back and loan it out at higher rates).

A Friendly Banker?

I had a friend who worked at a bank. Knowing that I was investing heavily in real estate, he approached me at a time when they needed someone to take over payments on a foreclosure. They made me an offer I couldn't refuse. The house appraised at about $160,000, but for $10,000 I could take over the payments with a balance owing of $70,000. I told him I didn't have $10,000 at the time. He said they'd loan me the $10,000 plus $9,000 to fix it up, with the payback at the end of the year. I was thrilled with the equity. He drew up the papers and when I went to sign I noticed the contract stated that the $19,999 was to be paid back in six months. I mentioned this to my "friend." He put his arm around me and assured me saying, "If you can't do it by then, we'll work with you." Well, at the end of six months they weren't in a position to work with me, so guess who lost control? (Not the bank!) I also lost most of the equity in that house. I lowered the price drastically and sold it quickly to get the bank out of my life and get myself back in control.

When staying in control is the name of the game you must stay away from the banks. There's a lot more I'd like to say about banks, but enough is enough.

Problem #3: Cashing Out and Uncle Sam

Other problems caused by cashing out concern income taxes. Most small investors need to be turning their properties in order to make a profit to live on. If an investor makes about $10,000 on each of three properties within a year, his income soars up into a higher tax bracket. The IRS may give some relief to the investor who holds a property for an extended length of time—long term capital gains. Sometimes, though, it's not in his best interest to do this. So, he sells and makes a healthy profit and reinvests the money in another place. Then, when he sells that, he makes more than he was planning on. Now *both* profits are taxed at an even higher rate. Trying to get ahead this way can be very painful. If he decides to rent for a while to take long term capital gains, he has accompanying problems that he may not want to handle. Without a doubt, this is one of the most difficult problems and is one of the main reasons why I've written this book. I will discuss the tax benefits of a new approach to investing in Chapter 10.

Problem #4: Rentals

On a cash-out investment, all of the profits must be claimed. But in order to save on taxes, some people retain their properties and play the rental game with its attendant problems. I have seen these problems destroy most investment plans.

The only alternative to this approach is to try a whole new way of investing in real estate. As a landlord I realized that this was just another problem that I wanted to avoid. (For more information on renting, see Chapter 9.)

Problem #5: Cash–Out Promises

Another problem is that of "balloon" payments. This happens when the seller absolutely wants his cash, but is willing to sell on contract with the whole balance (or a portion of it) due after a certain length of time. Ostensibly this is not bad. You may be able to stay in control if the balloon payment is not an extremely large amount or if you have enough assets which you can use anytime.

But I have seen many people not able to sleep at night because they felt so out of control. (This could be compared to the story I told about my banker "friend.") No one knows what the economy will be like when the balance becomes due a few months or a few years from now.

Problem #6: Inflation

Inflation itself is not really a problem when dealing in real estate. The problem that concerned me was, as an inexperienced investor, I centered my investment plans on it. Inflation can't be controlled; therefore, it's one of the problems I feel needs to be mentioned in this chapter. There were times I would invest in property with high hopes that it would increase in value by so much by a certain time. When that time came, I found myself in a dilemma because inflation didn't always do what I expected it to do. If I was counting on inflation to meet my promises, I was counting on something I couldn't control. Even if it increased beyond my expectations, I learned that this equity growth was not the same as cash—no matter what the increase. In other words, selling the property and getting at some cash is better than hanging on and hoping that inflation will increase your equity. I got tired of being controlled by this uncertainty, so, as I considered the profits in a piece of property, I only allowed inflation to be the icing on the cake.

Instead of trying to make money hoping that inflation will do what I want, I'd much rather find a good deal on a house. A deal to me is one where the owner *must* sell (for whatever reason), a house that needs a good cleaning (I'm surprised at how many people turn these down), or one that needs minor repair and cosmetics. This way, I am in control.

CONCLUSION

There seems to be a direct ratio between the amount of investing most people do and the control they relinquish to someone else. With others in control, the investor is playing an "away" game on *their* field and by *their* rules. An investor needs to play "home" games on *his* field and by *his* rules, so he can control his money.

During the first year of my investing, I was involved with all these problems—FHA/VA, banks, high taxes, rentals (tenants), and balloon commitments. These were the "away" team, and I was way out of my league. I needed a new ball game with a new set of rules that would let me be a winner. The name of the game is: **AVOID COSTLY ENTANGLEMENTS**.

CHAPTER **2**

The Solution

Have you ever been up against a brick wall? There's no budging it! That's the way I felt when dealing with the problems mentioned in the last chapter. I suppose I could have continued and I might have succeeded, but I kept thinking that there had to be a better way. I didn't have all the answers, but I knew enough to know that I wanted more out of my investing.

The investment plan I wanted had to answer the following questions:

1. Could I be in *control*? I didn't want any banks or government agencies telling me what, when, or where I could buy or sell.

2. Would it build a money machine that would give me a *continuous* monthly income?

3. Would I be able to slow down later? I needed something that would keep growing with relatively little effort.

4. Would it give me and my family *security*?

5. Could I *measure* my net worth and see my growth (without someone else's appraisals and conjectures)?

6. Could I leave assets behind for my family? I needed something that would be:
   a. steady and reliable

      b. inflation resistant
      c. easy to increase
      d. easy to handle

7.   Could I spread my assets around and not have them tied up in just a few properties or in one place?

8.   Could I invest quickly, taking advantage of current prices and conditions?

9.   Would I need to know everything there is to know about real estate or could I apply a focused knowledge to become effective?

10. Would it be challenging and exciting?

I analyzed what I had done with my first nine properties and at what other investors were doing. I realized that, if I kept going that way, it would be a long hard road to meet my goals. Sure I had made money, but I also paid a lot of taxes and was concerned about the future. The money I did make was at a great time cost. Then I asked the question, "What else could I be doing with my money or time?" The answer pointed me in the direction of reaching my goals.

Simply stated, the solution was **TO BUY AND SELL ON CONTRACT—ALL THE TIME**. If it sounds too easy to be true, it is - easy, I mean, and that's the truth! My properties and contracts have proven this approach to investing.

The next time I was forced to decide whether or not to sell another house FHA, I had to make a decision as to which direction I wanted to take, Had I sold the house FHA, I would have received about $12,000 five to six months down the road. My figures showed that I could sell the house on contract, get the down payment, invest it *again and again* and, at the same time, make it mushroom into $150,000, in equities which would net me $1,200 monthly. This idea demanded testing. It was a race to see what I could do within the next five months.

At first, it was business as usual. I took a $4,000 down payment and used it as a down payment and fix-up costs on the next house. Within a week I had it back on the market. It sold for $10,000 more than I had paid, I received $6,000 down. I also created an equity of $6,000 with a net income of $60 a month. It took five weeks from the day of my offer to close. Incredible? Not at all. Investors have done this before; the difference is that I committed to doing it this way continually.

I've told my story of playing "away" games and being out of my league. I wanted to take on someone my own size. After this deal I realized who that someone should be—not the banks, not the government, but other people. If I could work with people, I stood a better chance of controlling my progress.

There were four months left to see how many more times I could do it. With this $6,000 I paid some bills and purchased two more houses. Because we were dealing with people, and not institutions, we closed each of these transactions within two weeks. I had an offer from someone wanting to purchase one of these houses before I even signed the final purchase papers. They offered only $500 more down than what I had put down, but they were willing to pay $6,000 more than what I had just paid. I accepted their offer.

The other house needed cleaning. It had a few broken windows, and the yard was atrocious. Within four days it was manicured and ready to sell. That weekend I took an offer, and closed the deal the following Wednesday. Both of these houses were also sold within two weeks, only this time around I had $8,000 cash from the down payments and had created another $17,000 in equities with $150 a month coming in.

I was back out looking for more houses to buy, and over the next three months, I repeated this process eleven more times. I don't want to bog down this chapter with the specifics of these transactions; I'll cover many case histories in the following chapters.

At the end of the five months I had about $151,000 in equities and I was netting $1,290 per month. This investment idea passed the test with flying colors. (See Chart).

Let's see how it answered my previous questions:

A.C.E.

Avoid Costly Entanglements

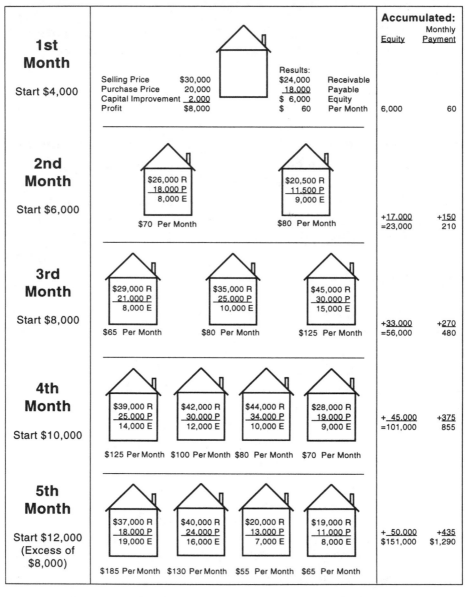

1st Month

Start $4,000

Selling Price $30,000
Purchase Price 20,000
Capital Improvement 2,000
Profit $8,000

Results:
$24,000 Receivable
18,000 Payable
$ 6,000 Equity
$ 60 Per Month

Accumulated:
Equity 6,000
Monthly Payment 60

2nd Month

Start $6,000

$26,000 R
18,000 P
8,000 E
$70 Per Month

$20,500 R
11,500 P
9,000 E
$80 Per Month

+17,000
=23,000
+150
210

3rd Month

Start $8,000

$29,000 R
21,000 P
8,000 E
$65 Per Month

$35,000 R
25,000 P
10,000 E
$80 Per Month

$45,000 R
30,000 P
15,000 E
$125 Per Month

+33,000
=56,000
+270
480

4th Month

Start $10,000

$39,000 R
25,000 P
14,000 E
$125 Per Month

$42,000 R
30,000 P
12,000 E
$100 Per Month

$44,000 R
34,000 P
10,000 E
$80 Per Month

$28,000 R
19,000 P
9,000 E
$70 Per Month

+ 45,000
=101,000
+375
855

5th Month

Start $12,000
(Excess of $8,000)

$37,000 R
18,000 P
19,000 E
$185 Per Month

$40,000 R
24,000 P
16,000 E
$130 Per Month

$20,000 R
13,000 P
7,000 E
$55 Per Month

$19,000 R
11,000 P
8,000 E
$65 Per Month

+ 50,000
$151,000
+435
$1,290

R = receivable contract   P = payable contract

Solution #1: Control

Dealing with people let me bypass steps that I would have had to go through with banks. I controlled everything and could sleep at night without worrying.

Solutions #2 and #3: Spin-Off Income/Keep Growing

Each of these properties (contracts) was giving me a net spendable monthly income. With a little creativity, I knew that eventually the plan would support itself. The hardest aspect of the plan was accomplished—that is, to have a perpetual monthly income and to have these assets spin-off enough income so I could slow down. The equities between my receivables and my payables did keep growing. (This will be discussed in detail in Chapter 12.)

Solution #4: Security

Security was another aspect that I thought would be difficult because questions about the economy kept coming up. Maintaining rental units had its advantages (which I'll cover in Chapter 9), but it was too unpredictable for me.

On the other hand, contracts provided me with everything I was looking for. They were secured by real property. In every case, the person making payments had something to lose if he walked away, the best incentive for keeping up payments.

Solution #5: Measurability

In real estate I've never found any form better than the contract for measuring my net worth. I had receivables (overriding contracts), payables (underlying contracts, mortgages, deeds of trust, etc.), monthly payments, and a way to delay my taxes (see Chapter 10 for details). I could measure to the penny what my net worth was.

Solution #6: Leaving Assets for My Family

Probably the aspect that gives me the most peace of mind is how this plan answers the assets question:
   a. There would be steady, reliable monthly income. (The bills come in every month, and it's nice to know they would be paid, even if something happened to me.)
   b. There would be resistance to inflation through the equity increasing as the underlying mortgages were paid off.
   c. Purchasing more contracts (see Chapter 20). My family could have my "team" help them to do this.
   d. Setting up collections through a good contract collection agency is a way to make contracts easy to handle— my family would receive just one check.

Solution #7: Spreading the Assets

This plan is emphatically efficient in this regard. In fact, I found that, in order to keep up the speed of the plan, I had to stay where the biggest market of buyers and sellers was. I could have gone for one big unit, but instead I processed five smaller ones in the same time and spread out my assets and liabilities.

Solution #8: Doing It Quickly

The results of my actual investing proved to me that it could be done quickly (e.g., 14 deals in 5 months). How well it worked in tight money conditions shows that it is a tenable plan—a great one for the times.

Solution #9: Being Effective

In Chapter 19, I talk about being a monomaniac. Success comes from targeting your efforts. I might not have succeeded as I did, had not my efforts been zeroed in on this one method. The simple aspect of believing in the plan and working to make it succeed created lucrative opportunities.

Solution #10: Challenging and Exciting

Because this approach to investing answers the last nine questions so well, it is probably the most exciting thing I have ever done.   When you've tried it, met the challenge and experienced the personal growth, you too, will agree.

KEEP ON TRACK

This investment approach does not preclude you from handling your houses in other ways, but I find almost strict adherence to this plan will bring success.   Once again, my approach is to process houses by always buying and selling on contract. Once in a while you will be tempted to deviate from this. If you do, make sure your reasoning is sound.

For example, I found a fixer-upper for $80,000 with $3,000 down. By putting $2,000 into it I thought I could get the value up to $97,000 (an additional $4,000 would get it to $105,000). In my own method I should have sold the house for $97,000, getting $5,000 down and going on to the next one. But I thought that finding another good deal would be too hard, so I decided to pour in the other $4,000 and gamble that I could get all $9,000 back when I sold the house for $105,000. Let's look at what happened to my thinking. (Usually in my seminars, I catch a lot of people smiling when I list the following. I think a lot of people have been here before.) The results will make you smile only if they are happening to someone else:

1. I felt that because I had put so much money into the house, I was justified in asking $105,000. The problem is, the increase in purchase price made it harder to sell.
2. Consequently, I had to make three more house payments before I could find a buyer.
3. I ceased to look for other good deals because my time was taken up and my money was gone. [Also, I lost whatever else my money could have been doing for me,]
4. To get my money back ($9,000), I had to require almost 10 percent down, thus limiting the amount of people that could possibly buy it.
5. I was left with having to sell it to some people who got conventional financing, and it took over six weeks to close.
6. I lost the right to claim my profit by the installment sales method.

MAKE DECISIONS FROM A POSITION OF STRENGTH

Once time and money were depleted in this project, I started making decisions from a position of weakness. Most wrong decisions are made at such a time. A house will take control of you when a chunk of you is in it. I thought this house would be the exception to the rule, but look what happened to my thinking process once I became deeply committed.

THE REAL ESTATE MONEY MACHINE

Get in control and quickly build up a lot of cash flow!

BIG PROFITS ARE REALIZED WHEN WE SELL!

I.   **Try to assume everything.**

Example:
1. Assume the existing loans
2. Create a mortgage (deed of trust) to pay seller's equity
3. Spend a small amount and fix up

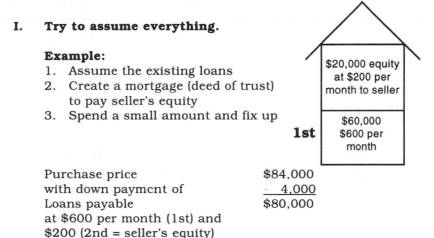

| 1st | $20,000 equity at $200 per month to seller |
| | $60,000 $600 per month |

Purchase price $84,000
with down payment of   -   4,000
Loans payable $80,000
at $600 per month (1st) and
$200 (2nd = seller's equity)

II. **Now sell on a wraparound. Try to get all of your down payment, fix-up, and closing back.**
House worth $120,000, but let's sell for $105,000 with $5,000 down.

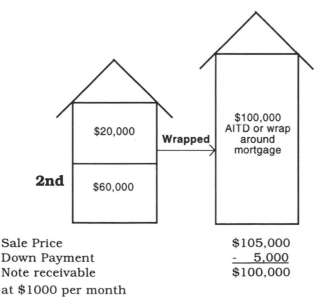

Sale Price $105,000
Down Payment   -   5,000
Note receivable $100,000
at $1000 per month

After a few years of using this new approach, I saw electrifying results. Suppose you could maintain buying and selling about two houses a month (it's easier than you think). It would mean that within two years you would have a net worth of just under $1,100,000 with an approximate net yearly income of $90,000. Before I write what the figures would be like in four years, let me state again: I was after the income that a million dollars could give me. All I needed to do was create the equities that would give me that kind of income.

Sure enough, within four years there would be equities of approximately two million dollars and the net yearly income would be over $180,000 or $500+ a day—including Saturday and Sunday.

I know this investment idea can bring you as much growth as it did me. The following chapters offer much of what I have learned over the past several years. It is given as support for this plan, constantly keeping in mind the ten questions, and the need to "avoid costly entanglements."

CHAPTER **3**

An Overview of the
Money Machine Concept

A while ago when I was writing my book *Real Estate for Real People*, I wanted to include a chapter on the Money Machine Concept. I wrote an extensive chapter. It said what I wanted it to, so now I am going to put it here to help you see the plan before you get into the specifics.

These past few years have been very enlightening. I've had the opportunity to be on several hundred radio and TV talk shows. At almost every one, the host has commented on my first book's title: *How to Build a Real Estate Money Machine*. The most frequent remark is that it sounds like a get-rich-quick formula. My usual comeback is that it is just the opposite. I tell the host that when I was writing the book, the publisher said, "Look, Wade, we've got a hundred books on how to make a million dollars, can you write a book on how to make a living?"

It took a long time to come up with that title. And even though only a few people have said it correctly when introducing me, every word does have its place. Money doesn't grow on trees, and it doesn't come from a machine. The concept, though, is to build an investment portfolio that continually gives off a monthly income with very little start-up capital.

It's fun to share this concept here in brief form. The book has done very well, and letters come in from everywhere, proving that a single concept repeated often enough will bring success. And once you've seen this concept, you'll realize two things: (1) It is true what the president of one company said: "I'd rather lose money and know how I lost it than make money and not know how I made it." If we can do something repetitiously, we can become good at it, refine it, analyze it, and retire on it. It's not that the job becomes easier, it's that our ability to do it becomes better. (2) This is no get-rich-quick scheme. It takes many long hours of learning and doing. There are many "no's" on our way to the "yes", but it is attainable, and it sure beats the alternatives.

That last sentence is a good diving board to get us into the pool. For a long time there were two philosophies for investing in real estate. One philosophy was to buy a property, fix it up, then find someone to get a new loan and pay you off. You then took the money and did it again, only this time with a larger property. You kept repeating this process. It still works today on certain properties, if they are purchased right. But the banks are too much in control, and it's almost impossible to stay on track, because the investor is not in control of most of the process.

The other philosophy is to buy and hold on to the property one day short of forever. Seminars teaching this method abound. This plan is also good if you buy low and get low payments, but it has two major drawbacks. The first draw-back is that it usually takes cash for the down payment and closing costs. Most people have enough to buy only one property. Then they have to save up or borrow to get a second down payment. The second drawback is becoming a landlord and having all the attendant problems. I've been there. It's hard to get started and find that all you ever do is make repairs. In today's marketplace there's so little profit (with the higher than usual monthly payments and rents that haven't kept up) that it seems as if landlords end up working for minimum wage.

The last thing I'll write about these two philosophies is that they just take too darn long. Most people get frustrated and give up. While the Money Machine concept is not a get-rich-quick scheme, it sure isn't a get-rich-slow scheme either. It is a sensible, proven way to make good money because it solves the need for a steady monthly income. Hard work is needed to build it, but then the money just keeps rolling in.

I'll spend the next several pages explaining the process and telling you what a few others are doing. But first it would be helpful to explain the concept in a few sentences. Test me as you read the pages after the next paragraph and see if I deviate. Everything is part of a puzzle. We can't go on to C until we've done B. Remember, repetition is the key.

The Money Machine concept is a system of buying good properties under market value with assumable loans, and hopefully, sellers who will take their equity (or most of it) in monthly payments. Then the properties are fixed up cosmetically and resold with the investor getting back the money put in and taking monthly payments for the newly created equity. The investor has created a lien on each property, and that is his security.

If that sounds like a mouthful, it is. But, like any concept, once it is explained and understood, you will say, "Aha!" It's like learning the secret to a magic trick.

BUYING

We have to buy right. The word "right" used here means that the terms and conditions of buying have to be conducive to selling. People often ask: "What if I can't sell it?" I truthfully reply, "Don't buy it." Only buy that which you can resell quickly. A good house in a fair to good neighborhood is the right choice. Buy in lower-middle-income neighborhoods. If you see people jogging, leave. Those are the wrong neighborhoods. Blue collar workers don't come home and go jogging. Blue collar neighborhoods are the right neighborhoods to invest in because they are where most people live. One other point: people getting rich and people getting poor have to live in the neighborhoods. We'll get them coming and going.

Buy houses with assumable loans. You're not going to hide anything from banks, so if they are going to be a problem, don't buy that house. Look for loans with an interest rate under 12 percent. FHA and VA loans are fully assumable. It costs a small name-change fee. There is no qualifying by you or anyone who may own the property in the future. We're obviously looking for diamonds in the rough. The old adage about buying the worst house in the best neighborhood is good advice.

Constantly be looking and have others looking for you. Carry a purchase agreement in the glove compartment, because good deals are everywhere. Keep in mind that, at first, finding these good deals seems like the hardest thing to do, but after a few weeks or a few months on the streets, this will be the easiest part.

The hard part is to find people who are willing to take monthly payments for their equity. Most people want cash. We need to get to people before they've mentally spent their money, so we can educate them on the beauty of monthly payments. I love monthly payments and would rather have $100 a month for twenty-two years than $10,000 cash, especially when I create the $100 from virtually nothing. If you think you'll have a hard time explaining to people why they should take monthly payments from you instead of a lump sum, you can show them a pamphlet I've written that explains all the reasons why monthly payments are beneficial. It's called "Owner Financing," and because it's only twenty pages, it will be convenient for prospective sellers to read. (If you want a copy, just send $4.50 to the publisher.)

Back to the process. The main thing to remember when buying is to guard your cash. When you sell, it has to be a good deal for the next person, and if you're demanding too much down, you won't find a buyer. When I buy, my average down payment is four percent of the purchase price, and when I sell, the average down payment I receive is six percent of the new selling price.

While "down payments in" and "down payments out" are important, the whole process bogs down if the monthly payments are out of line. When average people buy a property, they have to think about many things: the purchase price, the down payment, the monthly payments, the interest rate, and so on. Of these concerns, the monthly payment required either makes or breaks the deal. If this aspect is so important to the next person who will buy the house (or rent it for that matter), should it not be our number one consideration when we are buying? This is called "second-generation thinking." Most of us get bogged down thinking first generation. We just think of ourselves: how we like the house, how the monthly payment affects us, how we respond to the neighborhood, etc. Most problems in real estate investing wouldn't occur if the investor would think about the next person—the second generation.

We handle the purchase by the book. We use competent professionals to take care of details such as drawing up the papers, obtaining title insurance, and so forth.

use competent professionals

FIX-UP

The main idea, once again, is to guard our cash. If some people want to fix up a house to be fit for a king, let them. Instead, let's just do light, cosmetic work and general cleanup. The fix-up we do should be to enhance and sell the already good deal that we've purchased. Here are five general pointers that will prove the point. Others will occur to you when you get in the middle of a project and ask yourself the question: "What else could I be doing with my time and money?"

fix up to enhance

1. Fix up your houses for women. Women buy real estate. The final decision is theirs. I'm reminded of a story about a man up in heaven. There were two doors. One door was marked "For Henpecked Hus-

women

bands," and there was a long line of men standing in front of it. The other door was marked "For Men Who Are The Boss," and there was only one man standing in front of that door. When asked why he was standing there, he replied: "I don't know. My wife told me to." Women control the purchase of real estate.

2. Use one color of paint in all your houses and apartments. A nice, off-white is best. It goes with everything and makes small rooms look larger. Using one color will also save money because it can be bought in large quantities; moreover, you won't have a rainbow of leftover paint cans cluttering up your garage.

3. Don't dicker with your subcontractors on the price of fixing up. If you compromise on the amount of money you'll pay them, the quality of their work will go down.

4. Commit people working on your houses to an ending time for their work. If you don't, the job won't get done on time and guess who gets stuck with making payments on a vacant house?

5. Buy wholesale. You don't need a license. Just tell hardware, plumbing, and electrical stores that you're remodeling many houses and want to set up an account.

SELLING

So far, there has been a method to our madness. Everything has to make sense, and now that the property is livable, let's sell it. The terms of selling have to be a good deal for the next person. Many people are renting today because they can't afford the monthly payments. If people can rent a $100,000 house for $800 a month, why should they purchase it for $1,000 plus per month?

Every detail has to be fair. The down payment we charge has to be under 10 percent of the new selling price. We can charge more, but we'll probably have to wait. The interest rate

slightly under market value

should be under 12 percent, if possible, so the payment can stay affordable. The price should also be slightly under market value, so some profit is left for the next person. We buy low and sell just below high.

No one has ever written a book on <u>selling</u> real estate. I don't know why. In every other business, profits are made when something is sold. Granted, there are many advantages to holding real estate, but the selling aspect is so often overlooked. I contend that the way to faster profits is to treat the investments like a business.

I produced a seminar book and course entitled *Sell Your Own Property.* In it are hundreds of tips on selling: when to sell, when not to, how to structure the transaction, and others. But nothing works in the book and nothing works in life unless the selling of the property is a good deal for the next person.

Good Deal for next Person

This concept is not complicated. Your horse sense will get you over the hurdles. Map out a plan and minimize the obstacles. Why go to all this trouble? Because when it's time to sell, we want to have all of our doors open. We want to be able to sell the property in any way we please. If we've taken on a loan with a due-on-sale clause, many doors slam closed. If we put in too much money, the door of selling with very little down on a wraparound or assumption closes. Keeping all of our doors open takes cautious planning.

Remember, at some point you'll want to sell. Make sure all the terms and conditions of buying are conducive to selling. It doesn't take much to figure out that being cautious in buying the property and taking care to ascertain all future possibilities force us to make a good deal. Another case for doing things right is that doing them right works for us behind our back.

Just think of the alternatives—if we don't do this kind of planning and structuring, the results can be horrendous. Most of the problems I have experienced, or now hear about, have their origin in the financing arrangements for purchasing the property. If this is the case, then be careful. All of our

make Sure Buying is conDucive to Selling

efforts for good leverage and tax write-offs can go out the window with just one clause that restricts our right to sell. Be prepared to walk away from a bad deal that does this.

We don't want to create new problems by selling; we want to solve problems. Our first step is to see how selling will affect our other investments, especially our tax situation. It's amazing how fast selling one property affects the amount of taxes we would have to claim if we sold another one. We can go marching up through the tax brackets pretty quickly.

Real estate is so great because we are not limited to just one way of selling. It's fun because we can use different methods to solve different problems. We could hit a single (an installment sale for the entire amount, for example) and advance a little with very few tax implications, but with great monthly income. We could hit a double by getting some money down and carrying the balance. We could even hit a homer and get all of our money.

Perhaps we should wait for a while. The property might be a good rental unit, but the time to hit isn't right. We could even send in our designated hitter: switch the property for something else on a tax-deferred exchange. And it could be that after a few successful deals, we could take our mitt and ball and play a different game. I'm not recommending this—I'm just bringing up the possibility.

It's important and comforting to know that these selling methods are available. I suppose different ways have been developed with different tax savings, because so many people own and use real estate for their income, growth, and tax purposes. So let's explore some of the aspects of these ideas.

CASHING OUT

Sometimes cashing out is the most preferred method, especially if there is a lot of money tied up or there are huge equities. (For further ideas on huge equities and how to deal with them, see Chapter 16.) We can accomplish this by having our buyer get new bank financing. We can help out by quickly getting the information the bank needs, or we could possibly lend the buyer the down payment by taking back a second or third mortgage.

Cashing out has an effect on your tax bracket, so you should watch this. Make sure other strategies (i.e., holding properties as rentals) are in place. If not, you may have to pay some taxes. Remember, if you anticipate tax consequences, set aside the applicable portion so the money is there when the taxes are due.

These questions always come up: What else could you be doing with the money? Are you willing to play the game with the IRS or the banks to get the property sold? Will you benefit more with the excess cash? Do you have other properties that you can get into? Are they lined up and ready to go?

Cashing out is one of the greatest enhancers to any investment plan. From all of my experience, though, I have found that he who relies solely on cashing out hoes a long row. It's nice, but there are other alternatives. What I'm suggesting here is this: Don't go chasing after cash, but if cash comes chasing after you, take it.

INSTALLMENT SALES

This section is not designed to give all of the particulars of an installment sale, but only to give the highlights. I've covered the subject extensively in my other books. An install-ment sale is one in which you receive payments in two or more tax years. There are three advantages to such a sale:

(1) TAX SAVINGS. When you make a gain on a property you have to claim it, but with an installment sale you can claim the gain as you receive it. This means that, if you are receiving payments for twenty-eight years, then each year you'll claim the gain and pay taxes on it in that same year. The laws on this are changing, so see a good CPA.

How much you will pay is determined by figuring out the installment sales ratio for each property sold. Note: If the property qualifies for long-term capital gains treatment (currently, long-term tax laws are going through gyrations), then you'll only have to claim that amount. For example, if you bought a four-plex for $100,000 and sold it for $140,000 a year later, you would only have to claim a portion of the gain (current rate). In this case, it would be a percentage of the $40,000 gain, or about $20,000. (The exact amount is not hard to calculate.) This amount would transfer to your 1040 form through your Schedule D and affect your tax situation in some way.

If the property is held short and then sold on contract, mortgage, All Inclusive Trust Deed (AITD), or any type of owner financing, you must determine what you need to pay by figuring out the installment sales ratio. You do this by simply dividing the profit (or gain) by the selling price. (In this case it would be $40,000 divided by $140,000 = .286, or 28.6%.) This means 28.6 percent of the principal payments represents gain. The other 72.4 percent represents return of the cost basis (remember the $100,000).

Very few percentages come out even. They may carry out several decimal places. With the current tax law, you'll have to recapture any depreciation expense in the year of sale.

Now that the ratio is determined (and we use IRS Form 6252 to calculate all of this), we take that ratio times the amount of principal payments. This total is $1,200 ($100 per month x 12). We now claim a percent of this amount. Isn't this great? We've made a profit and have been receiving this annuity-type payment and all we have to claim is a portion. And it's this large in the first year because of the large down payment! If the principal received next year is, say, $720, then we would have to claim a percentage of this amount. As the principal part of the monthly payment becomes larger, then we'll pay more. Twenty eight percent will have to be claimed each year. But we'll have twenty-five to thirty years to claim our profit.

Note: If this property had been held for a long term prior to selling it this way, then even the amount claimed would qualify for long-term tax gains treatment. This rate may change each year, but the installment sales ratio will not change.

I realize this is difficult to understand at first, but after you've run through it a couple of times, it will become clear. Then as you understand and use this selling advantage, you'll realize what a great way to sell this is. You could actually create a fortune by "wrapping" properties and paying very little tax because you can claim the gain over the whole course of the loan.

(2) MONTHLY INCOME. The next great attribute of carrying paper is the monthly income generated by such a transaction. Money, especially big chunks of it, has a way of disappearing. These monthly payments, however, just keep coming in. Steady monthly income has always been my goal. Just think how nice it will be when you have several perpetual annuity checks in your mailbox every month.

Many people have asked me, "Why not get cash?" I say, "Because cash leaves right away." They ask about the present value and I ask what present or future value there is if the money is gone? One man told me he bought a new Cadillac with a chunk of money he received and then proceeded to tell me that all he had to show for it after a few years was an old Cadillac. Steady monthly income frees up your life. Ask anybody with payments coming in. I agree, the value of the money may go down, but so does the value of Cadillacs or anything else you may buy with it.

(3) SLOW AMORTIZATION. The loan doesn't pay off quickly, or early on, so the monthly payments will do little to reduce the principal. Therefore, you'll eventually receive an amount way over the contract price because of all the interest payments.

There are also other reasons. You can create these equity

notes and borrow against them, and you don't have to pay taxes on the borrowed funds. Imagine claiming your profits on the installment sales method and borrowing against the note! Now you have that money to invest or spend, or whatever. You could also trade these notes for other things— cars, property, or jewelry. The sky is the limit when you get creative.

Creative   Homes

PROPER DOCUMENTATION

This method of selling is called a "wraparound." It has become a very popular word, but many people still don't know what it means. It's just a piece of paper that creates a lien (loan) on the property. It is used to leave the existing loans alone. For example, I buy a house for $63,000 with $3,000 down. I assume a loan of $50,000 with a payment of $500 and give the seller a second mortgage or deed of trust for $10,000 and $100 per month. I put $1,000 into fixing it up and now sell it for $74,000 with $4,000 down.

I have received all the money I put in, and now I have a new buyer that owes me $70,000 with payments coming in to me of about $700. I do not let the new buyer assume the existing loans. We leave them intact. We do a wraparound. He owes me $70,000, I owe $60,000. He sends in a payment of $700, and I pay out $600 on the two loans.

Now, many of you may think this is complicated, but it just isn't. Hard, yes; complicated, no. I say that it's difficult because it takes a lot of time. Nothing comes easily. Finding the right property to sell quickly is obviously essential to the whole process, but it is being done by thousands of people all over the country. Some real estate offices around the country even have a name for it. They call it "cooking properties," after my last name. I'm grateful that it works for so many people.

One comment I hear everywhere goes something like this: "Wade, your plan is not easy, but it beats everything else." When I first heard this, and even now, I wonder why. They say, "Every other book and seminar out there tells us to buy and then rent. We can hardly ever rent the properties for what the payments are, and with your plan, we get higher payments when we sell, more security, and we also get all or most of our down payment back so we can do it again."

That's the whole point. It works because it solves so many problems. You have a need to build cash flow—this plan builds cash flow. You have a need to pay fewer taxes—this plan creates a tax problem, but it's spread over twenty-five to thirty years because you only have to claim your gain as you receive it. You have a need to maximize the return on your investment, and if done properly, you have no cash in. You put it in, get it out, create a note. (The New England states have a few obstacles to overcome in this as well as in any other plan. Some attorneys do everything and take their time about it. Out West, where escrow and title companies do everything, we can buy and sell in the same day.)

My average net monthly payment is about $195 per month. I had one that was $8 and one that was $290, but the average is just under $200. Most people can do this twenty or thirty times and retire. Just one property a month means that in two years, it's golf time. If you can do more, and most people do after they get familiar with it, so much the better.

By the way, most people think I'm crazy when I talk about doing something this quickly. But remember what Malcolm Forbes said: "No success is ever accomplished by a reasonable man." Besides, it sure is a lot more fun to go at something with intensity than to sit around and be bored.

Let me show you what I mean with the following story. I was in Buffalo in August. An elderly lady kept fidgeting in her chair in the middle of the room. It got quite annoying, and I finally asked her if she was okay. She said, "I just have to say something. You were here in May, and after listening to you, I thought you sounded a little nuts, but you looked like a nice guy, so I went out Sunday afternoon and found a little house I could buy. I didn't know how, so I went to an attorney on Monday morning and told him I wanted to buy it that day. He said okay, but it would take three weeks or so to close. I told him that I wanted it done in a few hours, that a man named

Wade Cook said that it could be done that quickly and, if not, to shut up and get busy." The audience chuckled at this point.

She continued, "The attorney said that it would take three weeks. He'd been an attorney for eighteen years, and it would just take that long. I told him that wasn't good enough, but to prove his point he called the title company to have them tell me it takes longer. They told him they weren't busy and could do it that morning. We did it by noon.

"Now, Mr. Cook, you told me I could do it in one day, and you also said I could resell it right away. I knew I had a good deal, so I went to a real estate office and asked if they had anyone who wanted to buy a house. They did. We showed it after three o'clock, and the man wanted the house. We went back to the same attorney, and his partner helped us wrap up the whole thing by five o'clock."

She concluded, "I'm making $82 per month now for eighteen years, then it goes up to $412 for the last ten years. I've done it eleven more times in the last four months, and I'm making $1,080 per month, net."

Everyone in the audience was staring at this woman. I, too, was taken aback. My mailbox is full of similar stories, but hers was exceptional. I then asked her if she would mind telling us her age. She said, "I'm seventy-two."

Don Berman said it best: "You can make money or you can make excuses, but you can't make both." There are people all over the country making what I did look like child's play. The concept is simple. Instead of going for the cash, we go for the cash flow.

I was standing in the back of a seminar room in San Jose, waiting to be introduced. A young man came up and, thinking he recognized me from my picture, asked if I was Wade Cook. When I said I was, he told me a very common story.

He told me he had gone to a seminar that teaches many ways to buy real estate, but nothing else. He bought two properties and had a negative cash flow each month of $600. He said, "I read your book and two days later I sold them and now have a positive income of $500 each month."

If there is one thing that I want to be known for, it is cash flow. When I die, I want my epitaph to read "Wade Cash-Flow Cook."

Letters come in from all over—testimonials to the fact that a simple plan done persistently will bring results, and big results, if you work at it in a big way. A man in Kansas is now the regional director for the western half of the state for the Boy Scouts of America, after following this plan for ten months and freeing up his time with steady income.

A woman in Syracuse is up to twenty-eight properties and had made $284,256 in about ten months. Another woman in Baton Rouge had $3,000 left from a life insurance policy on her husband, who had died a few years before. She had never purchased property before, but now did so thirty times in ten months. She has over $3,000 a month coming in, and this amount will increase for her and for everyone else when the underlying loans start to pay off.

I could go on and on, but you get the point. It works in Watts and on Long Island, from Seattle to Miami. The letters keep coming in.

If you put $2,000 down and get it back a week later (or a month later) and have created a mortgage with an income stream, your rate of return is infinity because you can't even measure it. You can't divide by zero. If you are lucky and find one for no money down and make $10,000 next year, you're at infinity again. If you learn how to refinance when purchasing and free up money when you buy (which is tax-deferred, by the way), once again you're at infinity or better. When I hear all of these people talking about a 28 percent return or a 100 percent return or even 150 percent, I say, "Don't talk to me about anything less than infinity."

CHAPTER **4**

" . . . Act, Act in the Living Present . . ."

There are two qualities that I've noticed in all successful people: one is the ability to make decisions; and two is being willing to take risks. "He who hesitates is lost" is too harsh for investors, because there's always another deal. It is true to a certain degree, though, because there is only a certain time period when deals can be acted upon. An investor has to be ready to move sometimes on gut feelings.

A few times, good deals ended up not being quite what I anticipated, but in the worst deal of all my transactions, I made over $4,000. I'm not saying that I couldn't have lost on any deal, but anyone who understands the fundamentals— and several alternatives—will not lose (unless there is really a bust in the economy, but even prophets of doom are buying real estate).

Let me compare investing to a torpedo. Once the enemy ship is in range, the torpedo is fired. The currents affect it and the enemy ship moves, but the torpedo stays on target. Why? Because it's constantly sending out radar signals that bounce back. When the torpedo receives this new information, it adjusts and corrects its direction. The battle would be disastrous if the captain of the ship said, "Why waste the torpedo? The ship will probably move and the current may be

too strong for it," or gave a hundred other reasons. Life is like this, but to the investor, waiting can be cruel. If a person wastes time trying to gather all of the facts, the deal will be snapped up by someone willing to move on it, having only the general facts and a feeling about the place.

On one occasion I saw a house for sale for $22,000. I called immediately and made an appointment to see it the next morning at 10:00 a.m. I made an offer of $20,000 with $1,000 down. He wanted $2,000 down, so I agreed to pay him an additional $1,000 in a year. We drew up the papers and went to the title company to have them notarized. While we were there I checked the status of the title. Seeing everything was okay, we recorded and said our goodbyes. I went back over to the house a few hours later, and there were five or six people in the kitchen. I said, "Hi, can I help you?" They asked me if I was the owner and I said I was. Then they said they were the ones that had called the night before and would like to make me an offer. I said "Oh, I'm not that owner. I just bought the house a few hours ago."

To say the least, they were quite stunned when I showed them the papers. They couldn't believe it, because they couldn't understand how it could be done so quickly, and why I was willing to buy a place that needed so much work—at least without getting bids to do the work.

These people had apparently come over the night before and, feeling good about the place, called a few contractor friends. (That explained the other people in the kitchen.) They were taking a magnifying glass to the house.

The man said, "But how could you buy it with all the work that needs to be done under the kitchen sink?" I asked him how much he thought the house was worth. He replied, "About $30,000." I told him I agreed. Then I asked him how much he would pay for it. He said, "About $20,000." I showed him that figure on the contract. Then I asked him how much it would take to repair under the sink and he said, "$500." I asked if he needed a contractor to tell him that. (He didn't want to answer because that particular contractor was standing right there.) I told him I estimated that the plumbing under the sink would cost $500, but I was also going to put in a new counter top and sink which would bring the total repair to $1,000. I concluded with the question, "So what if I only make $8,000 instead of $9,000 on the house?" He stood there scratching his head.

On another occasion I was standing in the yard of a vacant house with my heart pounding. This property was in foreclosure and I could get it at a fantastic price. I thought to myself, I've made between $8,000-$10,000 on all of my deals up until now. If this lady, the former owner, comes to sign these papers, I am going to make up to $20,000 on this house! Even though I had not seen the inside of the house (except through the windows), everything looked fine. (I had some questions, though. I couldn't tell whether it had three or four bedrooms, or how many bathrooms it had, nor could I tell if it had a full basement.)

I made an appointment to meet this lady at the bank at 10:30 a.m. and sign in front of a notary public. I left the house and drove across town, arriving about 15 minutes early. I sat there in my truck and waited. I tried to read a magazine, but couldn't concentrate because my heart was still beating too hard. I started getting nervous when it was 10:30 and she still wasn't there. I started thinking that she might not show because she knew she wasn't getting anything out of this, except ridding herself of the hassles of being foreclosed on. I was disappointed because this would be my one chance of breaking over the top and having enough money coming in each month to live fairly comfortably.

I decided to wait just a few more minutes. At ten to eleven I reached for the keys to leave, when I heard a knock. A woman standing at my window asked, "Are you the man interested in the house on Adams Street?" I almost knocked her over getting out of the truck. I had the papers all filled out and had previously checked the title status to see if there were any other liens on it. I was ready for her to sign. She showed her identification to the bank officer and signed the papers. After he notarized them we walked out. I said, "Listen, are you sure you don't want anything for the house?" She told me she didn't. I said, "When you purchased it a few years ago you put $98 down. How about if I at least give you your $98 back?" She agreed, so I gave her a check for $98.

I jumped in the truck singing and hollering all the way back to the house with the keys in my pocket. As I walked through the house I was pleasantly surprised. It was a five bedroom house, instead of the three or four bedrooms I'd expected. It had two full baths and a full basement. All this raised the value of the home and I figured it would sell for a price substantially higher than I had paid, with more down.

I called some people who were looking for a house like this, and they agreed to meet me there that afternoon. Because the house did need some new carpeting, the people offered me only $4,000 down, so they could keep the other $1,000 for carpeting. I accepted their offer. We drew up the earnest money agreement, took it to the escrow company and closed the transaction three days later. They moved in the following weekend.

This is a deal where I put down about $2,000 out of my pocket (to cure the back payments), and took a little time to check the title status of the property. I took over all the loans on the house. When I sold it for $4,000 down, I had net monthly payments coming in at $140. Had I waited to gather all the facts, the foreclosure proceedings on this house would have finalized. The risk was there, but so were the profits.

VOLUME BREEDS HIGHER VOLUME

Moving on deals like this quickly put me into a different category. I knew that speed was important, so I hired a few employees and a subcontractor to do the work on some of these houses. Each house was a race against time.

Right when I decided to slow down, a realtor called and said she knew of eight good houses. I told her I was too busy and couldn't handle any more, but she persuaded me to go look. We spent the afternoon checking them out, and I made offers on all eight. Because I was so busy, and only wanted to handle them if the deals were really right, my offers were almost ridiculous. She went to work and within three days she had five of them locked up. The last one was sold by the time she got there.

I knew that I needed a big exit if I was going to buy this many. I needed to be able to sell them quickly. (Some of them needed to be sold before I finished buying them.) When she told me I was the proud new owner of seven more houses, I was shocked. At first I didn't know what to do—I never thought they would accept. Now I had to work quickly so I could turn them into profits.

Before I tell you what I did with them, let me tell you some of the terms on the seven houses. My average down payment was about four percent. They let me assume over $100,000 at less than eight percent money —$40,000 of it was less than six percent. Not one house had a "due on sale clause;" for that matter, there weren't any clauses that would restrict me when I went to sell them, either.

Five of the seven houses were livable right then, needing very little work, and were sold within three weeks. The other two took two months to fix up and sell. When they were all sold, I had $84,000 in equities and was netting $750 a month. I paid the estate agent out of some of the down payments and I still had $6,000 cash left over.

The tide rose in my life right then and I felt it was time to ride it. I was able to squeeze in all this excess activity because I learned how to process and sell the properties. That information is still valuable today and no book anywhere contains it. One learns it, out there, by doing.

Let me illustrate this point: I had a friend who wanted to do what I was doing, so he spent a week with me. During that week I rented one apartment and one house, put ads in the paper to sell two houses, looked at ten houses to buy, and made earnest money offers on four and bought two of them, evicted a tenant, met with three subcontractors on a number of jobs, fired an employee and hired a new one, and picked up a house on foreclosure for about one-third of its value.

At about 4:30 PM on Friday we walked out of the courthouse where we recorded several deeds and I said, "Well that's about it—you've seen what I do." He clasped his hands together and said, "Boy! I've got to take some college classes and learn how to do this!" He had missed the whole point. There isn't such a class. You learn by doing, by acting, by taking chances and by being aggressive.

To summarize, I'll quote the last stanza from the poem that served as the title for this chapter:

> "Let us then be up and doing
> with a heart for any fate . . .
> Still achieving, still pursuing,
> learn to labor and to wait."

Henry Wadsworth Longfellow
A Psalm of Life

CHAPTER **5**

This One's on the House

For the past two years, I have had the distinct pleasure of traveling the width and breadth of this country. In every city, there are people trying to get ahead. Some are trying to make a little extra to cover bills, some are looking imminently at retirement, and almost all are discouraged by the huge tax bite taken out of their paychecks.

I've listened to their problems, their concerns, and their successes. I've seen literally hundreds, possibly thousands, become wealthy. <u>Everyone did so by taking his own life into his hands and making things happen.</u> Nobody handed any of these people anything on a silver platter. They worked hard for everything. The free enterprise system is alive and well for anyone enterprising enough to stick his neck out.

I hope that I have been a help to some people. My original goal in turning to this field of education was to help people see new ideas, try new avenues, and find a more excellent way of doing things. People from all over have consulted with me by phone, in letters and in person, and I take this responsibility very seriously. I've always tried to make sure what I teach and write is useful, pertinent information.

Often I'm asked, "What do I do now?" "I've heard you speak and I'm excited Mr. Cook, but what do I do first?" Or

"Mr. Cook, can you give us some advice in just a few words?" To all these questions, there must be one good answer. Yes, every person is different, but there is one piece of advice that gives support and direction to everything else we do.

THINK BIG

I've searched long and hard for such an idea. I've watched real estate investors go through the good, the bad, and the ugly. Finally, I thought I was getting close in the early part of 1983, but before I wrote about it, I wanted to try it out on audiences in many states. I got excited about this idea, and my desire to express it sharpened as the economy started to recover. People were confused. "Is now the time?" "When do we get started?" "What area of investment is best right now?"

The idea was well received. It is not for the high rollers, but for the average person who wants his actions to mean something. I've also discovered it is consistent with every-thing else that I've been writing and teaching. It's amazing how the puzzle fits together. Well, here it is in all its simple glory: THINK BIG IN A WHOLE BUNCH OF SMALL WAYS.

Many of you have heard me and know the emphasis I put on the "Z" of any system. The Z is the end, the retirement. It is where we want to end up. Once we know where we want to be, we can set up systems to get us there. The "think big" of this idea is just that, and a little more. We need to think ahead, plan and then work. We need to know what we want each property to do for us. We must understand how it fits and what we are trading off by buying, renting, or selling it. The alternative to thinking big isn't a very comforting thought. I can say that, because I can pretty well guess the type of person who is reading this book. Many people are content to live mundane lives or to be victims rather than participants in life. But not you. You want to get ahead as fast as you can, yet cautiously, and I commend you for your desires.

Thinking big—at least dreaming big—is a way of life. It's easy to get bogged down and lose sight of our goals, but we are in control of our destiny and that's the place we need to be. Thinking big is what gets us out of bed earlier in the morning, and it's the element of our character that gets people to follow us. You'll learn quickly how important those other people are. Think high and fly.

The Numbers Game

The next part of the idea is the "whole bunch" concept. Whatever you're doing successfully is strengthened by doing it time and time again. The one thing that I've learned about business success is that there are no secrets. Success is achieved by obedience to certain principles. There are hundreds of laws, but they all fit into three categories: fill a need; work hard and think hard; and play the numbers game.

Playing the numbers game is what I want to write about the most. It doesn't matter what business you are in, all you need to do is figure out the numbers game for that business and you'll be a success—eventually. Once you've figured out the game, then figure out your modus operandi and get to work making it happen.

You've probably all heard something like: "I look at 15 houses, make offers on six and buy one." The numbers may change but the concept is the same. You cannot control the "one," only the fifteen. If you want the "one" to happen, you have to look at the fifteen and make offers on the six. Playing the numbers game also keeps you in control. You're not spending all your time looking at and negotiating on one house, but on many. The good deals will come.

What does this mean in the context of this book? I will present many ideas here on the beauty of investing in single family houses, with a focus on creating systems and only doing that which can be duplicated. It is sufficient to say here that repetition breeds success. No athlete ever wins a gold medal without first training, time and again, beforehand.

If we are doing a whole bunch of things and creating systems that help us duplicate our successes, then we have a jump on our future. Not only is the repetition bringing in money, but it also allows us the opportunity to refine the system. It gets better and easier with practice.

We're all convinced that real estate is the best vehicle for wealth accumulation. (If not, may I suggest you read my book, Real Estate for Real People.) We need more real estate deals to solve our problems. Thinking big doesn't mean thinking about big deals. It means thinking of attaining goals; that is, finding attainable properties that help us reach our goals.

For those people who ask me questions about where to start and what to do, I answer emphatically, "Invest in single family houses." Single Family Houses (SFH) or small rental units should be the backbone of our investing. All the following chapters answer the why's, how's and what now's. I sincerely hope these concepts bring into focus many of the ideas that have left people befuddled. Now is the time to be investing. Suit up! It's time to hit the waves—not tidal waves, but the little ones that we can handle. Think big in a whole bunch of small ways.

Why Single Family Residences?

It would be good to ask the question, "Why single family houses?" There are several good answers which we will explore. However, it is beneficial to realize that there are many great forms of investment. An investment is as good or bad as the problems it solves or creates for the investor.

With this in mind, the first question that needs answering is not "why" but "for whom does the doorbell ring?" If you have plenty of money and are in a "preserving mode," then single family houses may not be for you, although you'll see several aspects of investing in SFH's that will help even you. If you are in a growing mode or accumulating mode, then read on. These words are for you.

Let's divide investors into two groups: big and small. The big investor is usually where he is because a lot of small investments were used as stepping stones. Moving from small to larger investments is usually a matter of time management. No sense monkeying around in the minors if you're ready for the majors (but please read on).

The other investor is the small investor. The rest of us fit into this category. We are the small investors who need more income, more wealth accumulation, and more tax write-offs. We've read a book or two on how to get ahead. We may be making $10,000 a year or $100,000 a year and it's still not enough. Our investment assets are usually under $100,000, but commonly in the $150,000-plus range. This chapter is written for those people or companies who need to grow as fast as possible with as little cash involvement and risk as possible.

Why single family houses? The first reason is an outgrowth of the fact that there are more small investors than large. If I can establish the fact that SFH's are good for the small investor (and that will be easy to do), then it naturally follows that investor demands for SFH's help to increase their value, even causing them to be a great investment in all other SFH areas.

The demand for such dwellings goes further than just investor demand. Most people desire to own their own piece of earth, and we know "they ain't making no more land."

But why single family houses rather than multifamily houses? The next reason rests more on the small investor's own knowledge and locale. These houses are just down the street, next door or across town. It's easy to gain knowledge of areas, prices, and institutions to deal with. SFH's are everywhere, which means good deals are everywhere. Remember, the goal is to be in control. You're not waiting for the Dow Jones industrial average to come out or the London gold exchange to close to know how you're doing. Add this to the fact that most small investors already know a great deal about real estate. Most people have bought and sold a few of their own houses or have been tenants. All of us have seen the good and the bad of real estate investing, and this knowledge can only help.

The demand for individual housing is still here. Obviously, the culprit in slowing down housing is high interest rates. Look what happens when long-term mortgage rates get close to 12 percent. When interest rates drop to 10 percent and under, this demand will show its head like never before. Bad times force people to get smart, and the one thing everyone learns is that Congress loves real estate. This has extensive applications for the investor. The homeowner realizes these savings and so does the real estate investor.

Because Americans place high value on home ownership, SFH's remain the best possible form of investment—bar none. And the smaller the unit the greater the number of people wanting it. Single family houses stand head and shoulders above their closest competitors.

MORE BENEFITS

There are many other areas of discussion that explain further the benefits of investing in single family residences.

- A whole industry is set up that deals with single family houses: bankers, builders, real estate people, title and escrow people, lawyers and CPA's; not to mention the suppliers of material and services. These business people need each other. Prices are protected. Laws are created. Tax incentives are installed. Anything you need to know is yours for the asking. All this helps the small investor.
- With the creative purchase techniques in practice today, especially those that let you maximize the laws of leverage, an investor can buy several different

properties to solve different problems. He can buy a duplex for tax write-offs, three houses to build cash flow on the money machine concept, and a four-plex to fix up and cash out of. It's great to be diverse with so little money.

- Once you purchase many houses, you learn many ways to keep doing it. We need to be able to analyze our methods. The only way to do that is to do things that can be duplicated. I'm not saying to buy duplexes or three bedroom houses alone, but to set up systems that can be re-created. For example: every morning from 7 to 8 AM, look at the paper for good deals and call on at least five ads. Every afternoon from 2 to 4 PM, meet with an agent to look at and make offers on properties. This may be a lot of activity at first, but after a while you can cut back and not work so hard. Get the working the system, then refine it. No area of investing lets us do this better than single family houses. And once you get "the goose that lays the golden egg," don't kill it by changing.

- The last point that I'll mention here is that once you own any investment and then decide to unload it, you need to have all your options open for doing just that. With SFH's you can cash out and get your equity, then trade your equity for a different property— perhaps a larger unit that you can start depreciating at the new price. Maybe you want income without the rental headaches so you can take your equity on a note. This way is also good if receiving the cash would force you into a higher tax bracket. You could lease it on a long-term lease option and hold onto the tax write-offs, possibly getting higher-than-average rents in the meantime. If you need cash, you may want to refinance and pull out your money that way; later on, you can sell, trade, or refinance again.

Yes, these investment benefits are available on larger units, but for the small investor, SFH's will allow him to build assets faster and take more advantage of owning and selling. Think big in a bunch of small ways and think big in a bunch of diverse ways.

Author's Note

In the next few chapters I'll mention examples of houses in the $30,000 to $50,000 price range. This may seem low for some areas of the country. The Money Machine works in 1996 in Newport Beach or 20 miles away in the Watts area. One area has houses averaging $180,000; the other, $25,000. There are many cities with an abundant supply of houses priced under $50,000.

CHAPTER **6**

You Have to Buy Right to Sell Right

How angry would you be if your foundation collapsed and your house was ruined? A proper foundation is essential to buildings. It is also essential to any investment plan. Investing in real estate can do one of three things: save money (by using depreciation expense, tax shelters, etc.); make money (by finding good deals, improvements, inflation, etc.); or, lose money (by not laying the proper foundation).

If the following conversation happened in a store, we would applaud the store owner.

"But nobody buys anchovies any more."

"Come on, you only have to order a case to get this special price. They'll never be at this price again."

"I don't care what price they're at. Nobody buys them, so I don't want them."

The salesman leaves. The store owner maintained control —he knows what sells and what doesn't. Should investing in real estate be any different? Should we be any different from this store owner and not know the exit before we go in the entrance? Investing in real estate demands that we know the exit or we will flounder by not moving deliberately and quickly enough to succeed.

Let's compare selling property to getting a rebound in

basketball. After all, the house is on the rebound. You need to be in the right place to get an offensive rebound and make a basket. In real estate there are several things you can do to get yourself in a wrong place—a place where it's hard to shoot from. Then you might have to: (1) take a bad shot, (2) pass off, or (3) lose the ball. The best thing to do in real estate, like basketball, is to eliminate the obstacles.

The foundation of my idea is simple and solid. George Washington probably said it best when he said, ". . . avoid costly entanglements." Most investment formulas that I've read keep the aspirin companies in business, but by following the advice in this book, we will all have fewer headaches.

Avoid Promises You Can't Keep

The most common costly entanglement is making promises that can't be kept. Don't think that you have to buy everything you see—good deals are always there. If a certain house has an uncertain future, avoid it. The most common promise (which will cause a foreclosure if not kept) is agreeing to pay additional cash at some future time. This is not bad if all your bases are covered, but if you are relying on some future event, especially inflation, then you might end up behind the eight ball. I've been there several times.

One time I found a house for the low price of $10,000. I was to give them $1,000 down and $90 a month on contract. At the last moment they received an offer for $10,000 cash. I thought I was going to lose the house (I knew it would be worth $30,000 all fixed up), so I offered them $15,000, if I could pay them in one year and pay nothing down at the beginning. They accepted. An additional $5,000 dollars sounded good to them. I got the house habitable and rented it. When it was time to fix it up and sell it to cash them out, I didn't make the needed money. They started legal proceedings. I was able to save the house and make a little profit, but it was a totally unenjoyable experience. As a matter of fact, looking back over the several years of my investing, every really bad experience I had was when I committed myself to perform in a market I couldn't control.

Short Versus Long

It reminds me of a football game where all the pass receivers go short, the quarterback drops back and passes long—and no pass is completed. Property investments are usually for the long run, not the short run. If an investor gets caught borrowing short and selling long, he will get trapped. Or if he invests his short-term money in long-term projects, he will soon run out of cash.

Many times I would borrow fix-up money from a bank. Almost invariably something would go wrong, some delay or some change that I had no control over. The loan would become due and I would have to get extensions and sell other properties. It got to the point where I wanted no short-term money. It caused too many headaches.

I know this sounds harsh. After all, there are all kinds of books on using OPM (other people's money). If you are just getting started, go ahead, but be careful. Remember, their expectations are probably different than your expectations. Stay in control. Be prudent. Promise only what you can control.

PROPER FOUNDATION—PART I

The number one concern is that the property is being purchased at a good price. You're investing to make money and build a future. Keep that in mind. If the price is too high, even if all other factors are okay, reconsider the purchase. Does it fit into your plans?

If a property needs to be resold quickly, buying at a good price is mandatory. Selling quickly will happen only if you can resell at a fair price. If you can stay just below the medium income housing bracket (where most buyers are), it will sell easily.

My economics professor had another good story, a little facetious, but instructive. He said, "If you want to be successful, sell food or women's shoes. Everyone needs to eat, and the average American woman owns 26 pairs of shoes." He had considered real estate, as well, because everyone needs shelter. His lesson was to go where the market is.

One other important point needs to be covered. I'm a firm believer in not overcharging. When I price my houses, I leave enough room to raise the price if the prospective purchasers come in with less down.

For instance, I had a house that was worth $50,000 tops. I put it up for $48,000 with $4,000 down. This is sound investing, in that you're not trading the other things your money could be doing for you by leaving it tied up in the house for a long time.

Don't Bury Your Cash

Buy with a low down payment so you can sell at a fair price and recover your money. Don't compromise, hoping inflation will bail you out. Make sure it's worth your while. It takes a long time for great terms to make up for an overpriced house or too large a down payment.

Keep your cash turning. Don't bury too much of it. In the preceding example I put $3,500 into this property. Sure, I now had $9,000 in equity with $80 a month coming in, but I had buried $1,500 of hard cash ($3,500 minus the $2,000 down payment).

I went through a four month period when I did this seven times. I was putting entirely too much emphasis on equities and not on what it takes to continue growth. By the end of this time, I had run out of cash. It was all buried in equities.

PROPER FOUNDATION - PART II

Make sure all of the terms are agreeable and assumable. Either on the Earnest Money Agreement or on the contract, you will make promises to the person selling you the property. He might want all kinds of things. Some of them might not seem bad at the point of purchase, but, at the point of selling they could destroy the deal.

Some glaring clauses to watch out for are:
1. Due on Sale clauses
2. Payment Acceleration clauses
3. Clauses limiting your right to sell or encumber the property
4. Usurious interest rates
5. Excessive late payment or early payoff penalties.

Most of these are reserved to the banks, but as they get more prevalent, many people begin to act like banks and want similar clauses. Read contract details carefully, even if you are told that it's a uniform contract.

PROPER FOUNDATION - PART III

Payments should be kept low, as should interest rates. If someone wanted to charge bank rates I would remind him that he is not a bank and therefore should look at what the banks were _paying_, not _charging_. This is good advice. When selling, the same basic principles should be followed. (I've met people who tried to get every last penny. They didn't last very long as investors.)

The process of deciding on the payment amount always starts with questions because nobody knows how much to give or take. If I'm asked, I say jokingly, "I would like to pay a dollar down and a dollar a month for the rest of my life." It might sound stupid, but at least he knows where I stand. Once again, if the interest rates and monthly payments are too high (even assuming all else is okay), it will be hard to sell and generate any kind of cash flow. For instance, if you are paying $300 per month on a $20,000 loan and sell the house with a $30,000 balance with payments of $300, you'll have no cash flow (but a great equity growth). Only do this after you've built your income and have a lot of experience.

PROPER FOUNDATION - PART IV: LOW DOWN

This can't be emphasized enough. The more money you sink into a place, the less control you have over your selling options. Having to recover large amounts could dictate the way you have to sell, even when the taxes will kill you. Guard your cash.

Sometimes you'll need to rent. We'll cover that in Chapter 9. If you do, the best rentals (tax-wise, leverage-wise) are the ones that tie up the least amount of your money.

Location in Perspective

The phrase, "What's important to business? Location, Location, Location," takes on a semblance of importance, but I'll add this: anything will sell at the right price. Of course, houses will sell for different prices, depending on their areas of town, but profits are everywhere. You should be aware of this intangible information and know what you are getting into.

Don't Make His Problem Your Problem

I went to look at a house owned by a guy who had to "unload" it. He purchased it for $20,000 and started making extensive repairs. This may seem like a low price in light of today's prices, but the house was a wreck. Nothing worked— not the plumbing, electricity, or heating. He ripped out walls, started lowering ceilings and began stripping all the trim back to wood. To this point he had made it uglier in order to make it more beautiful, but it was uglier. He had already spent $5,000 fixing it up, but then ran out of time and money.

After listening to this story, I said, "Look, I really sympathize with you. I'm sorry that you read someone else's investment formula and then couldn't make it work, but the house is still worth only $20,000." That's what I offered. He wanted to sell it for more, but after two weeks, he called back and accepted my offer. It would have been easy to let his problems become mine. We all want to help, but *I didn't want to make his problems my problems.*

CONCLUSION

In summary, get all the terms compatible with the ability to resell the property quickly. Even one catch or disproportionate promise could jeopardize you. If all the terms are not in line with your best interest, go on to something else—don't compromise.

I have traveled extensively all over the country and have spoken before thousands of real estate investors. Many have asked if this same plan can work in today's market.

Let me preface my answer with this comment. When I travel, some people say the houses I talked about in the $80,000 to $100,000 range are too low for their states. The next week I'm in middle America and people complain that I'm talking too high. I know some who are buying 2-5 houses a month and have never paid over $50,000 for any of them.

Does it work? The answer is emphatically, "Yes." As a matter of fact, other investors are making what I've done look like kid's stuff.

People have taken these ideas and started fresh or have used these ideas to fine-tune what they are already doing. They have done it with nursing homes, shopping centers, apartment complexes, condominiums, and even storage units.

Several have devised ways to get back several thousand dollars on the down payment turnaround.

It's like anything else; it is the active doer who achieves success. There are plenty of reasons for failing in real estate investments and many dwell on those reasons. They don't do anything but get good at excuses. Investors who continuously proceed will win the prize. It is gratifying to see so much happening with these ideas. It worked for me and to see it work for others adds a special dimension.

CHAPTER **7**

Tips on Buying–Part I

Give Them What They Want,
But in a Different Way

A concept to help you buy right and sell right is give them what they want, but in a different way. This assumes that the purchase arrangements are not exactly compatible with your plans and rather than lose the deal, you need some alternatives to present to the seller. Once again, your only limitation is your own imagination. I developed this concept over a period of time by trial and error. Developing it was necessary because deals slipped away when I couldn't satisfy the need of the seller.

A Seller Who Knew What He Wanted and Would Settle for Nothing Less

One summer day, I came across a five-plex that was just what I wanted. The selling price should have been around $80,000, so when the seller said he would like to get $57-$59,000 out of it, I said, "It does need a lot of work, but $57,000 sounds like a good price."

"But I have to get $8,000 down," he demanded. I didn't

have that much cash, but this was no time to walk away. Stupefied, I asked why. "Because I have $4,400 in back taxes on the place and I need $3,600 to pay some bills." Now I had a bargaining point. In that county, taxes could be five years delinquent before there would be a tax sale.

I had plenty of time before that so I asked, "Would it be okay if I pay the back taxes later and pay you the $3,600 now?"

He said, "Okay, but I have to get $500 a month on the balance and not a penny less."

"That's a good payment, but how would it be if I give you $350 a month for a year, then $450 a month for the next year and then $550 a month for the whole balance of the loan?" He said that was okay.

We drew up papers that weekend and it was mine for $3,600. I had given him what he wanted, but on terms compatible with my plans. And because I bought right, I got by with putting a mere $3,600 into it, and after 15 months, I sold it for $120,000 with $15,000 down. My payment coming in was $1,000 and the next year my payment going out was $450.

He felt satisfied because he had made me give him what he wanted. I hadn't disagreed with him, but had agreed quickly and then changed it a little to suit my plans.

The Seller Had Plans But Could Wait for the Money

Another time, I received information about three houses for sale on one piece of property. The owner wanted $30,000 for all three, but she wanted too much down. I asked her why she needed so much and she said she was buying into a dog kennel partnership and would need $5,000 on January 1 of the next year to do it. Add that to the $2,000 for closing costs, and the required down payment was at $7,000. She also had a $7,000 underlying loan with a $250 monthly payment at 8 percent interest. (This payment was too high for the loan amount.)

I brain-stormed with the agent to come up with the
following offer: The purchase price would be $27,000. I would
pay the $2,000 up front. Then on December 1, I would pay the
other $5,000. I would assume the $7,000 loan and pay her
equity of $13,000 at $200 a month starting 30 days after the
$7,000 loan was paid off. Interest at 9 percent would also start
the day it was paid off. In other words, she would let $13,000
sit dormant for five or so years with no interest at all. She
thought this was great—and for her it was. First, she was
going to get her money in time; and second, she wouldn't have
to be a landlady anymore, which she hated.

The foundation was in place for a good resale. I put $3,000
into roofing and minor repairs, and then sold all three a few
months later for $59,000 with $5,000 down. Payments
coming in were $550 per month. My payment was $250. I
could have used the $5,000 down payment to pay her off, but
there were other uses for it right then, and there were still four
months before December 1. In November, a few other deals fell
through that I was to use to pay her. This contract was too
good to sell but her money was past due, so I had to sell it. The
people that bought my contracts ate this one up. They
couldn't believe $13,000 was sitting dormant. My equity was
$34,000 which was the difference between my receivable of
$54,000 and my payable of $20,000 ($7,000 + $13,000). I
received $24,000 cash for this equity and after paying her
$5,000 note, we cleared $19,000.

All of us—the seller, the agent, my buyers, and I—got what
we wanted, just in different ways.

FIND OUT WHY THEY ARE SELLING

People sell properties for good reasons. It's so important
to find out the "why" behind their selling. You won't be able
to offer alternatives until you know what they need.

A friend of mine made an offer on a house that required
$2,000 down, which was more than he wanted to put into it.

Upon inquiring why that much was needed, he found out that the seller wanted to get his daughter a car for about $1,000. He quickly offered his wife's car, which the man took as credit for $1,000. His wife was angry for a few weeks—until he sold the house and bought her a newer station wagon, which she loves. He also made enough to get two more houses.

Are There Alternatives to What They Think They Can Get?

A Realtor called about a possible triplex. The zoning was right, and each possible unit had an outside entrance so it wouldn't take much to turn this turn-of-the-century house into three separate units. The seller wanted $82,000. I offered $80,000. I hadn't yet learned to assume all underlying loans or take the property "subject to" the existing loans, so my financing was a straight contract payable at $775 per month. The morning it was to close I thought I'd be home in an hour.

At the escrow company I found out about an underlying loan I hadn't known about. Then I found out she was having all kinds of financial problems. I wanted nothing to do with making a payment to her and hoped she would pay the underlying payment. (Even though there was plenty of protection against this in the contract, I just didn't want to be bothered with it.)

We changed the papers for me to assume the loan and pay her the difference. Her equity payments were going to be only $140 a month at five percent. Because the underlying payment was so high, her payment had to be smaller, and in order to get the payment this small, the interest had to be substantially reduced. She agreed and was even relieved that she wouldn't be responsible for making that payment. But she started crying when she saw that my whole $4,000 down payment was eaten up in closing costs and all she would get was $300. After making changes, we were ready to sign, when her agent felt that these changes should be reviewed with his broker. We agreed to meet at his office and close there.

While driving, I kept asking myself, "Why was she crying? What does she want?" By the time I got to the office, I figured out that she must need more cash now. After the broker agreed with the changes, I offered a different plan that I had devised in the car—which was for me to pay all the closing costs, her back payments and back taxes and give her $2,000 right then. They wanted to talk it over.

I sat out in the car for 30 minutes and when the broker came out he said, "She accepted your second offer, but with one change." Reluctantly I asked what it was. "She wants the $2,000, but because she is going through a divorce, she wants $1,000 of it now and $1,000 in 60 days." Of course I accepted. The price was lowered to accommodate this change and therefore, so were the closing costs. As a matter of fact, the money required to close right then (partially because I delayed the taxes) was $200 less than the previous plan. She was elated to have the money and I returned home with the place for $73,050—not the $80,000 I was willing to pay for it.

Excellent financing was now in place. And because such a low price and terms had been negotiated, I wouldn't have to put that much more into the place for a good profit. I had the lawn mowed and the home cleaned up and then put it up for sale one week later as a "triplex fixer-upper." It sold in two days for $96,000 with $7,000 down. I made back my original capital plus the $1,000 to pay her. Then my contract equity was $10,000 with a net monthly payment of $105. Everyone got what they wanted.

Ads in the Paper

"Home for Sale" advertising usually tells very little of what's important to put a deal together. Occasionally, you'll see "Leaving town, must sell", but even that is rare. Also, only a few of the acceptable terms are in the ad.

I have made some of my best deals from what looked like hard financing. Read past the words. Don't be afraid to make suggestions. You never know what someone will take. And what they won't take today, they might take next week.

Once I offered a man his $2,000 down payment at $200 above the regular payments each month for 10 months. He balked at first, but later called and said, "Make it $225 and you've got a deal." At times I approached a seller about a contract and he agreed to sell it that way, even though he originally demanded cash. For a detailed brochure of many of these techniques, see the *Available Materials* section in the back of this book.

Creating User–Friendly Wording

Some sellers think they will not be able to enforce contract terms or that certain wording is slanted in the buyer's favor. Take the wording, "A $15 late payment will be assessed if payment is not received on or before the due date." This can be put in user-friendly terms, i.e., "It is mandatory that the purchasers make this monthly payment on the due date. If not, they will have to pay a late charge of $15." Yes, they say the same thing, but the second sounds more comfortable to some people.

CONCLUSION

Continuously look at houses and the deals will be there. Of course, you won't be able to get compatible terms on every house you look at. If not, move on to the next one. But if you are creative and persistent, you'll make good deals where others don't. Giving them what they want, but giving it to them your way, will lay the foundation for success.

"If there's a way, take it; if not, make it."
ANONYMOUS

CHAPTER **8**

Tips on Buying–Part II

Get There Before the Crowds

This subject is probably the most often written about subject in real estate. Whole books are written on it, so I don't want to belabor it here. I will just cover the basic premise and then give a few tips.

Common sense tells us that if several people are bargaining on the same house, the price goes up. It's the old law of supply and demand. In every city there are different ways to get there first. Do some research and find the system that works best for you. For a long time I chased foreclosures. A few of the best deals I made were on foreclosures, but after pursuing several of them, it got to be very nerve-wracking. Some other investors I knew specialized in them and were extremely successful. It wasn't comfortable for me, so I went in other directions. Here are several suggestions for any investor.

THE REAL ESTATE AGENT

A real estate agent can be an investor's best friend. A good agent, who is looking out for your interests, will probably be your greatest asset. I had one agent who knew what I was looking for. He combed the city, watched the paper, called other real estate agents and offices, knocked on doors, and kept going over the MLS computer (see note on MLS computer). Within three months, I bought eight properties through him, and they all met most of my requirements.

I've had several agents working for me at one time, but once in a while it caused friction. One good agent is more valuable than ten mediocre ones.

If you want to find a good real estate agent, call a real estate office and ask to speak to the broker. Tell him, or her, that you would like to work with the broker or one of the more experienced agents. This way you have a better chance of getting agents who know what they're talking about. After all, if they help you accomplish your goals, they'll be accomplishing theirs.

Remember, there is good and bad in every profession. If you find yourself with someone who is slowing you down, you need to move on to someone else. Once you find a good real estate agent who recognizes your needs and your goals, hang on to him—make him your friend. His help will be invaluable.

Get a good agent, then make sure he understands exactly what you're looking for. Let's see how he can help you get there first.

It's the nature of their work to search and look for properties. Real estate offices fluctuate between:

1. Having all kinds of listings (and therefore having a few good deals).
2. Having few or no listings (meaning they're out looking for sellers, and they often uncover good deals).

Real estate agents are able to hold a listing for a few days before it has to go into the computer, so during that time they might try to find a buyer on their own. If I could find a real estate agent holding a property, it usually represented a good deal.

I would walk into an office and ask them if they had any

good deals in their back pocket. If they pointed toward the computer, I'd leave, knowing they had nothing. I found several "pocket listings" that led to investments in this way.

A Note on MLS Computers

Be a little leery of the MLS computer. Remember it's only as good as the information that's fed into it. Real estate information is hard to keep current because people forget to update.

One day, a new real estate agent showed up with a computer printout of thirty houses. I couldn't believe there were so many. I spent the next two days looking at each one. The terms weren't right on most of them, but I was ready to make offers on six. Then I found out that four of them were sold — one of them three months earlier and one two months earlier. One of the last two had an offer on it that was better than mine, and the other seller didn't accept my offer. Neither the agent nor I did the right homework. Two hours of phoning would have saved two days of hard work.

FORECLOSURES

Probably the best deals come from distress sales. There are several ways to find them:

1. Watch the legal notices in your local paper. In larger cities, there is usually a paper dedicated to such notices. You'll find them under "Trustee's Sale," "Sheriff's Sale," "Foreclosure Notice" or "Tax Sale."

2. Contact attorneys who handle trustee sales or probate. You'll see their names in the trustee notices. Sometimes they are reluctant to give out information on other foreclosures, but if you're nice and persistent, you'll find them.

3. Realtors can sometimes assist in finding foreclosures.

Once you find a foreclosure, follow these steps:

STEP 1:   Go look at the property—the address should be in the notice. If it's not, call the attorney and ask, or get it from the title company. Seeing the property will enable you to assess its value and get an impression of the neighborhood, etc.

STEP 2:   Call the attorney in charge. The property may have been "cured." If not, he or she will point you in the right direction and reaffirm the cure and sale dates.

STEP 3:   Find out from the bank or the attorney, the balance on the loan and how much cash is needed to cure the deficiency, back payments and costs. Most of this information is in the notice, but often it is not current.

Before going on, let's review what will happen if the mortgage is not brought current. On the appointed day the attorney, acting as trustee for the bank (beneficiary), will stand in the courthouse lobby or on the steps and announce his intentions. He will then bid the total amount (balance of mortgage and costs) on behalf of the beneficiaries. If no one else bids, the sale is over and the bank can then take possession and dispose of (sell, hold, etc.) the house to recover its money. Any excess money received on this sale goes to the owner. Also, any other bidded amount needs to be in cash (or cashier's check) right there at the time of sale.

One other point: Each state (and some counties) gives homeowners a certain period of time to redeem their interest. It could be six months to a year. During that time, they could come up with the previous amount due, plus current charges and interest, and thereby get the house back (even if it had been sold). The redemption right is usually only on sheriff's sales, but check into it. Basically it means the investor could have money tied up for that period of time. If the previous homeowner comes up with the money, then the investor's money is returned (plus a modest amount of interest). Also, the previous homeowner could convey that right of redemption by using someone else's money and then selling the house to them. These could be good deals, but be cautious.

STEP 4: Check the chain of title to see if there are any other liens on the property. Also, check the person's name at the title company to see if he or she has the right to convey ownership unencumbered.

STEP 5: Get to the homeowner before the property goes past the cure date. Before that time, you could pick it up for the back payments, plus a few hundred dollars in costs. Buying it at the trustee's sale will require the whole loan balance, foreclosure costs, etc. — in cash.

Once you meet with the homeowners, you will see the frustration of this system. Usually the house is vacant and it takes some detective work to track down the homeowners. If you can find them, they're usually willing to convey the house because it will protect their credit rating. A few people would only convey if I gave them a few hundred dollars. The most I ever paid was $800. Point out to them that they have probably already lived in the house for the last four to ten months free (not making payments) and that you're using your cash to cure the default and to clean and fix up the house. If the people are still living there, it's even sadder. They can't believe they're losing their house. (One foreign-speaking lady wasn't even aware of what was going on.) I usually explain the situation, state my intentions, and then leave, giving them my card so they can contact me. Often they won't do anything and then, after the sale, they're evicted—still not believing that this could happen to them.

STEP 6: Have the homeowner sign a Quit Claim or other appropriate deed. Also, draw up an agreement stating what both of you will do, i.e., move out, clean up, hold harmless.

STEP 7:   Notify the bank and the attorney that you wish to
cure the default and they will tell you what needs to
be done.

NEWSPAPERS

This is probably the most often used service for selling
houses, so it could be your best place to find good deals. Don't
think there will be a hot deal every day. Maybe once a week
a good opportunity comes along. But keep looking.

Call and ask questions about financing. See if you can
make a good deal out of one that ostensibly doesn't look too
promising. I go through the "Homes for Sale" section and
circle the ones I'm interested in. I start calling on the ones that
I get excited about. Call first, even if the address is there; it
will save you a lot of gas. If you're actually looking for your
next house, try to get the paper as soon as it comes off the
press and act right away.

ADVERTISE YOURSELF

Put out some form of advertisement to let people know you
are in the market to buy houses. I once put an ad in the paper
which read, "I'm a young investor looking for houses to buy,
to fix-up and sell, or to use as rentals. Call _____." I didn't
get a lot of calls, but the ones that did come in were rewarding.

I ran that ad for two weeks. Just before it expired, a man
called and described his house, which had been damaged in
a fire. He invited me to look at it. He had already received his
insurance money and basically wanted me to take over the
mortgage.

I took over the mortgage of about $50,000 on the house,
which was in one of the nicest neighborhoods in the city. I
realized that this house had a lot of potential and would be a
great one to fix up and sell for a profit.

I poured about $10,000 into the house for repairs and monthly payments. I sold the house for $127,000. So that ad did work. All it took was one phone call to make a small fortune. I run the same ad from time to time, and once in a while I receive a profitable phone call.

Another ad has gained popularity lately: "I will pay full price for your house if you will be flexible on the terms." Even though I like the way it reads, I think it would be safer to make it read, "I will give you good terms if you will be flexible on the price." The first has a guarantee that you'll pay the price, which might increase by the time you get to the house. The second ad only guarantees good terms. Because terms are arbitrary, you can go out and negotiate a good deal.

Even when you aren't actively looking, keep something going. *Good deals usually don't come looking for you; you have to go looking for them,* **all the time.** Keep the wheels in motion and the gears greased.

Once You've Found the Property

The next step is to make certain all the terms are compatible with your plans. Don't think that the seller should be deprived of his rights in order to go along with yours. Be fair and realize that sometimes a good deal can't be made. Never buy a property without an earnest money agreement, or some other agreement, stating what is expected of all parties.

One of the biggest headaches I ever had was on a deal with no earnest money (or agreement). The buyers were supposed to do certain things, but it happened so fast that we just drew up the final papers. Then, when they didn't perform, all I had were verbal promises. I thought they would come through so they could keep the property, but they didn't. They walked, and I was stuck with a much worse situation than before.

I've purchased several places for little or zero down. In many cases, though, the seller is willing to take a small down payment for some kind of trade, say, a cash-out provision, a higher price or higher payments. I know of some investors whose best deals, in terms of low downs, turned out to be their worst deals in the long run. They made promises they couldn't keep. Guard your cash. Be careful not to promise that which you can't give. Other people's money is usually short term, and if not repaid promptly, their patience is also short term.

Speed is the word. Do what it takes to get the property sold (or rented) as soon as possible. The following might help. When you're going to sell it right away, the one thing that will hold up the transaction is getting title insurance, so order it immediately after you purchase the property. Then all you'll have to do is get an update and you could close in a matter of days (or hours) rather than weeks. Also, remember that it could sell at any time, but it is very unlikely to sell if it's a mess. After you've ordered the title report, get the lawn mowed and clean up the yard. If the grass is long, it takes two to three weeks after cutting before it's green again. Mow it even before you finish buying—that's not too much of a financial risk to take. Even if the house needs repair, it could be sold right away if it's clean inside and out.

I bought a house once that was *so cluttered and dirty* that all the floors had to be raked before they could even be swept. After fifty large sacks of garbage were taken to the dump, I could see a 100 percent improvement. Another look and I knew I'd made a much better deal than I'd originally thought. The seller had even admitted earlier that he'd had a hard time finding a buyer because it was so filthy.

Most of us go through a thinking process that takes a while. When there are so many possibilities for every house, we need as much time as possible (preferably someone else's time). If the house is vacant, get the keys upon acceptance of the earnest money. Don't put any money into the place until it is legally yours, but at least you'll have the keys to look at it (and possibly find someone to buy it from you). A clause for the earnest money agreement should read, "Purchaser gets keys upon acceptance of earnest money."

I used to go over to a house early in the morning and lie on the floor. It was quiet and I could look around and go over all its possibilities. I missed those experiences later when I was processing many houses at once. Fewer mistakes were made during that time, and I could also get bids on work that needed to be done and get everything ready to go.

Gut Feelings

It is important to be a little intuitive when buying places. Other people's formulas have to become yours. Adapt them to fit you, because you're the one who wins or loses. Sometimes certain things about a property outweigh the figures in a formula. Gather as many facts as time will allow, then trust your feelings. If you have properly prepared yourself, things will go well, probably even better than you expected.

Publisher's Note

Mr. Cook has written a book entitled <u>How to Pick Up Foreclosures</u>. This book explains the facets of the foreclosure process. This book also contains a questionnaire that will help you focus on the process used in your home state. This questionnaire alone could save you thousands of dollars. The goal of the book is to get you to the purchase point of houses long before the auction. We're confident it will help your investment process. You can order this book by sending $16.95 to U.S.A. Publishing, 24837 104th Ave. SE, Suite 201, Kent, WA 98031 or calling 1-800-872-7411 if you have a Mastercard, Visa, or American Express. Please add $3 for postage and handling.

CHAPTER 9

A Comparison of Investment Strategies

"Wait a year, then sell it," has been said so often that it seems like it's the only answer to protecting one's money. While the IRS has contributed to making investing in real estate lucrative, it would be unimaginative to invest with only tax ramifications in mind. Do not ignore the IRS and plunge headfirst into any type of investment and then look back and see what tax implications your actions have had. What I am saying is that everything should be viewed in proper perspective.

For example, if you were to buy and sell a place and make $10,000, you might have to pay several thousands of dollars in taxes. Should you not do it then? Proper tax planning is important to minimize your tax liability, but when tax considerations keep you from acting in a profitable way, then it's time to step back and take a look at your progress. This chapter will help put this in perspective and help you answer the question, "What else could I be doing with my money?"

THE IRS AND YOU

Note: I'm going to try to make the following information on the IRS sound as good as possible. Don't stop reading, though, until you've finished reading the three projects at the end of this chapter.

Depreciation Expense

The first consideration is depreciation expense. It means you can recover the total cost of a building over its useful life. For example, if you purchase a building for $114,000 (plus land value of $25,000) with a useful life of 27.5 years, you will be able to take $4,145 a year depreciation expense, which will help you shelter your rental income, plus any other income. This example is figured on the straight line method.

$$\frac{\$114,000}{27.5 \text{ years}} = \text{over } \$4,000 \text{ per year}$$

But you have to use the IRS chart, **Make sure your CPA is familiar with real estate**. If, on this building, you have a net profit of $2,000 for the year, $4,000 will be applied to that, and the difference (a $2,000 loss) will show up on your 1040 and offset other income.

If you do repairs to the building which add to its value, this will be added to the cost basis and will also be depreciated over the useful life. This is a problem to some people in that they want to deduct all of these repairs in the year they were done. But if they are considered capital improvements, they will have to be added to the cost basis.

Leverage

Probably the biggest benefit of real estate compared to other forms of investing is that property can be purchased with only a portion of the sale price as a down payment. Ten percent financing is common, but there are many cases of purchasing properties with little or zero down. In any case, these tax benefits add to the rate of return on your money. The less money down, the greater the return. For example, if you put $5,000 down on the $114,000 building, in the first year you recover about $2,000 of the $5,000 in cash. That's a great return, and if you are in a 28 percent tax bracket, you will save another $560 (28 percent X $2,000) by being able to deduct the excess depreciation expense against any other income you might have.

Long–Term Gains

The second consideration is long-term capital gains realized upon the sale of a property. Congress did away with these gains for many years, so they have not been a consideration. As they are reinstituted and go through their gyrations, it becomes IMPERATIVE to keep current on your tax knowledge.

Before you claim them, you'll have to adjust the cost basis to account for the depreciation expense that you've already claimed. You may not deduct depreciation and then not figure it back in. Depreciation expense reduces the cost basis so your profit is actually larger. Because you have held it long term, you'll only have to claim a percent of that. That's pretty neat—you've made a profit but only have to claim part of it.

There are other forms of depreciation which will enable you to claim larger amounts in your early years of ownership. Remember that when you recapture these amounts, any amount claimed on the straight-line method will have to be recaptured.

If you hold on to this building for several years, you will continue taking the depreciation expense each year. When you sell it, the profit will be claimed at long-term ratios. This is not a major concern because of the advantage of claiming these gains on the installment sales method. This is a point that most investors overlook. They continually subject themselves to the headache of landlording, when, with hardly any tax liability ramifications at all, they could be making more money.

Increase in Values and Rents

The third consideration, already briefly covered, is the increase in value and the likely increase in rents (if rent controls don't kill these increases). The value is increased by improving the building and by inflation. All of this is a tax advantage while you own the property, in that this increased value is only figured in at the time you sell the property.

You can see why many people buy rental units; there are many advantages. The few negative aspects can be taken care of with caution and planning.

Negative Cash Flow

The first negative aspect to rentals is cash flow. If expenses eat up your income, it could cause hardship. Make sure you can financially handle more going out than is coming in. Even if the tax advantages are available in the future, make sure the financial situation won't harm you in the present. Yes, even with a negative cash flow, the other tax advantages are there, and your tax advantages are probably heightened. However, this negative cash flow will eat into the money you've targeted for other things. You will also have an increased hardship if your tenancy rate fluctuates.

On Being a Landlord

The second negative aspect of holding longer is being a landlord. I've spent many hours tracking down tenants, fixing toilets at 2 A.M. and trying to figure out who's growing those funny weeds in an upper unit, etc. I don't like being a landlord. Fortunately, there are property managers around who can handle this and free up your time so you can be an investor. Be sure to find a good firm to handle this. They should help you "avoid costly entanglements."

There are excellent books on all of these subjects, both positive and negative. It's not my intention here to go into detail, but only to lay a foundation. When we get to project number two (dealing in rentals), the result will be clear.

PROJECTS FOR COMPARISON

We're going to hypothetically invest some money three different ways. The time period will be one year. All three projects will start with $4,000.
- The first project will determine how much cash we can turn by buying, fixing up, and cashing out as many properties as possible.
- The second project will be to take the $4,000 and buy a rental unit.
- The third project will be to buy on contract, fix up and sell on contract as many times as possible.

All of the properties are actual transactions of mine - I've used all three of these approaches. After you study the following, it won't be hard for you to see which approach I use exclusively now.

Project #1

Cash Out

Purchased : Jan
Sold: May
Net Profit: $7,500

Purchased: May
Sold: Sept.
Net Profit: $8,500

Purchased: Sept.
Sold: Dec.
Net Profit: $9,000

Results

1.   Profit $25,000.
2.   Taxes to be figured at 30 percent (for simplicity's sake)—$7,500 netting $17,500. We won't figure what effect this tax bracket had on other income. It should, however, be figured in real life.
3.   All three were handled through banks, with their attendant problems.

Project #2

Buy A Rental Unit

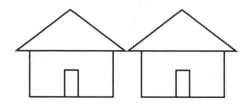

Purchased duplex for $60,000
$600 Monthly rents
$550 Monthly expense

The payment mentioned here doesn't include the principal part of the monthly payment. The principal is not expense.
$50 x 12 months = $600 net income

Results

1. $600 cash in pocket (principal paid totaled $400, so actual taxable amount equaled $1,000).
2.   Property value had increased to $66,000.
3.   Rents should increase next year.
4.   Depreciation expense of $2,182 (27.5 year straight line) offsets the $1,000 profit and the excess depreciation expense can offset other income (30 percent tax bracket x $1,182 = $354 added savings).

5.   If and when sold, the amount over your adjusted basis of \$60,000 + Capital Improvements is taxed at long term rates.

Sounds good, doesn't it? But wait until Project #3!

Project #3

Months	Equity	Monthly Payment
1.	\$ 6,000	\$ 60
2.	23,000	210
3.	56,000	480
4.	101,000	855
5.	151,000	1,290
6.	184,000	1,560
7.	222,000	1,970
8.	244,000	2,280
9.	298,000	2,800
10.	340,000	3,200
11.	364,000	3,420
12.	392,000	3,680

Buy and Sell Contracts—All the Time
Avoid Costly Entanglements—A.C.E.

(Author's note: The results of this project are so superior to those of projects one and two that had I not made it happen myself, I would find it hard to believe).

Before we determine our final equity, the following needs to be considered: during the year, three people who purchased my houses fixed up and sold the properties, cashing me out. I used that money and sold two other contracts to invest further and pay the taxes.

Results

1.   Equity of $310,000 (several people cashed out during the year.)
2.   Monthly payments (net) = $2,800
3.   Cash on hand $17,000—generated from our excess down payments and a few of the cash-outs.
4.   Actual net cash received from the monthly payments during the year totaled over $12,000.
5.   Equity growth each month now totaled $890 (the increasing difference between our receivable balance and our payable balances).

I started investing by borrowing $500 from my father, and at the end of one year I actually had $4,000 and started the A.C.E. Plan. I was building a *Real Estate Money Machine!* I never realized that such a small amount of money could grow into so much. All that I ever wanted in any investment plan was knocking at my door.

WHAT ABOUT THE TAX BENEFITS OF RENTALS?

I don't want to diminish the importance of depreciation expense, long-term capital gains, etc. During this time I also had several rental units that helped me avoid paying taxes on the small amount I had to claim by qualifying for installment sales consideration. (See Chapter 10 for more details on taxes.)

You might be asking yourself, "If buying and selling on contract all the time is so great, then why would you want to have any rentals at all?"

The answer is simple. I want to retain as much profit as possible. I do believe in paying taxes, but I want my tax burden to be as light as possible, so I structure my investments to avoid and defer as many taxes as possible.

In order for my tax load to be light, I needed to take an "eight cylinder approach" (See Chapter 15), using all appropriate deductions to my advantage. I'm not saying that I went out in search of rental units. I actively worked my plan, but when I came across a good property for renting, I would buy it for that purpose.

What constitutes a good rental? There must be hundreds of answers to that question because so much is written about it. My answer centered on "avoiding costly entanglements."

High Leverage

First, I wanted hardly any of my money tied up in a rental unit. So the down payment had to be small and the fix-up cost low. If this were not the case, I would borrow against the property to free my money up again. If this couldn't happen, it was back on the market for sale. Remember the results of the three projects. Having my money dead-end into a rental project for over a year in no way compared to the advantages of keeping it moving.

Positive Cash Flow

Second, it's becoming increasingly hard to find properties where the rents cover the expenses, but they are out there. As I said before, I wouldn't go looking for these units, but if they came along and all the monthly figures were right, then, and only then, would I buy to rent.

Property Management

Third, I'm an investor—not a landlord. The property had to be easy for someone else to take care of, with all the traditional rental aspects being in line, i.e., vacancy factor, location, yield rate.

CONCLUSION

You just need to look at the results of the three projects to see the differences. All were successful, but to increase your success, even above the normal lucrative aspects of real estate investing, use the A.C.E. concept as your primary focus of attention. I've never seen any other investment plan work so well. However, I am not asking you to change anything you're doing or forget anything you've learned, only that you "up" what you're already doing.

If you're just getting started, then "go for it," but if your plan is already in motion, then use these ideas to get your investment elevator to the top floor. Add it to what you're doing for synergy.

CHAPTER **10**

Tax Advantages

All through this book I mention the tax advantages of selling on contract. When I started using this approach, this wasn't one of my major considerations. But after setting up several good contracts, I questioned the method of claiming profits. I knew I would have to claim the profits, but since I wasn't receiving that whole amount at one time, I wasn't sure what to pay. About this time my accountant was reviewing my financial situation. He said, "You really like this, don't you? You get to buy a lot of places and create these great contracts, and you get your money back so you can do it again — not to mention these monthly payments."

The answer to his question was "yes," but it became an emphatic YES when he said, "Wait until you see the tax advantages you'll receive for doing it this way." I wanted to shield as much as I could from the IRS, but I didn't think it was going to be this good.

The installment sale tax techniques have gone through several gyrations. Most tax advisors have not kept up with the changes. I've spoken to dozens, and not one has had a handle on the current law. Find an advisor who is up on the law — preferably one who invests in real estate. In the meantime, the following questions and answers will help clarify the tax scene.

Q. What is an installment sale?

A. The sale of real property priced over $1,000, with payments made in two or more tax years.

Q. If I do many transactions this way, am I likely to be considered a dealer?

A. Yes. The laws regarding this have changed. Check with your CPA or United Support Association, Inc. for an update.

Q. Can I receive more than 30 percent of the sales price as a down payment and still qualify for these tax advantages?

A. Yes. The law has been changed, so now the seller can receive any amount as the down payment and still qualify.

Q. Why is claiming profits this way such an advantage?

A. Because it lets you spread the payment of your taxes out over the length of the contract.

Q. How do I know how much to claim?

A. On any sale that qualifies for installment sale consideration, you claim only the portion of any principal payment received which represents profit.

Q. That sounds exciting. Tell me how much I will have to claim this year on the following sale: I purchased a house for $30,000 (nothing down) and put $3,000 into fixing it up. My selling expenses came to $2,000. I sold it for $50,000 with $5,000 down. I received payments of $450 for 12 months of which the PRINCIPAL portion totaled $1,000 for the year.

A. You will pay that portion of the $6,000 ($5,000 down payment plus $1,000 principal from the monthly payments) which represents profit. (See Example 10-1)

Q. Won't I have to claim my whole $15,000 profit?

A. Yes, but over the entire course of the loan.

Q. How do I figure that?

A. The easiest way to figure it is to use the IRS Form 6252 that you'll see in Example 10-1. In this case, your profit on the house is $15,000. You divide that profit by the contract price of $50,000 and you will get the ratio to use when figuring how much to claim. $15,000 divided by $50,000 = .3 or 30 percent. This year you will claim 30 percent of the $6,000 that you received. (You claim only $1,800.)

Q. Do you mean that I was able to recover my invested money, create a $15,000 equity contract netting $150 a month (12 x $150 = $1,800 each year) and all I have to claim is $1,800?

A. Yes.

Q. What about next year?

A. That 30 percent ratio will continue for the length of the loan. Let's assume that the portion of the monthly payments which is principal totals $1,200 next year. You then would claim 30 percent of that, or $400.

Q. Are there ways that I could avoid claiming even these modest amounts?

A. Yes, even though you'll have to claim it, there are ways to shelter it. In Chapter 9 we went over rental units and long term capital gains. I'll let my explanation there answer the question.

Q. Where do I put this on my tax forms?

A. Come up with the figure each year on Form 6252 and transfer that amount to Schedule D.

Q. Schedule D—isn't that the form for Capital Gains?

A. That's right. This transaction could also qualify for long-term capital gains, which means that if you held this property for over six months, you would have to claim only a percent of the gain. Back to your example: This year you would only have to claim a percent of the $1,800.

Q. Will I only have to claim this percent of the 30 percent each year?

A. Not necessarily. Even though your profit ratio doesn't change, the IRS might change the capital gains exclusion. Each year could be different. (See examples 10-2 and 10-3).

Q.   What happens if my buyer makes additional principal payments?

A.   Those payments are treated just like regular payments. The portion representing profit is claimed.

Q.   I've just figured the ratio on the sale of a house and it involves a lot of numbers after the decimal point. How many numbers should I use?

A.   Seven or eight. That might seem strange, but in order to get the figure on Line 19 correct, you'll need them all. (See Example 10-5).

Q.   When I sold my house I maintained the underlying mortgage. A friend said my profit was the difference between my payment coming in and my payment going out. Is this true?

A.   No. The amount of monthly payments coming in and going out has nothing to do with the profit of this transaction. They also have nothing to do with the ratio. These amounts (profits and ratio) need to be calculated according to the simple way explained on Form 6252.

Q.   But is the interest paid deductible? And doesn't the interest received have to be claimed?

A.   Interest is interest and has nothing to do with capital gains. Interest income is treated as ordinary income and must be claimed. (The amount goes on the front page of your 1040). The interest expense can be a deduction and is reported on your Schedule A.

Q.   What about the amount of principal coming off the underlying loan?

A.   It has no tax bearing.

Q.   What do I do if I have claimed depreciation expense already?

A.   That amount would be subtracted from your cost basis. You won't be able to claim it twice. (See Line 9 on Form 6252). One additional note: Take all the depreciation expense you can. Being able to reclaim it here, especially if long-term, is a great way to avoid paying taxes.

Q.   I bought a property and refinanced it. When I sold it, my cost basis was $63,000. The amount of the refinance loan was $73,000. I did this to free up some cash. Then when I sold it, I let my buyer assume the loan and pay me my equity on a second note. What do I claim now?

A.   You'll have to figure your profit ratio and apply it to any principal payments received. But in this case, you will also have to claim the amount by which the assumed loan is greater than your cost basis. Here it will be $10,000 ($73,000 assumed loan and $63,000 cost basis). In this example, you are still able to spread out your tax liability, but you will then have to claim the percentage of your principal payments that represents profits.

Q.   How can I avoid having to claim this assumed amount?

A.   Don't let your buyer assume it. Carry a "wraparound" contract for the whole amount. Note: Line 6 on Form 6252 takes for granted that the buyer assumes the underlying mortgage(s). If this is not the case, write in "mortgage not assumed." (See examples 10-1 and 10-6).

Q.   Can you give me an example of a transaction where more than a 30 percent down payment was received?

A.   Yes (See example 10-6).

Q.   What happens if a subsequent buyer cashes me out?

A.   Your ratio has been established. All your profits at the percentage would then be claimed.

Q.   What happens if I use my contract equity for a trade?

A.   It is added to the cost basis of your new property no matter what ratio it is traded at. For example, the person selling you the property may only give you 70 percent of the contract value.

Q.   How do I claim my profit if I buy a contract? I purchased a $10,000 mortgage for $6,000.

A.   You figure this the same way as before. Divide your

profit by the contract amount—$4,000 divided by $10,000 = .4 or 40 percent—forty percent of all PRINCIPAL payments will be claimed as they are received.

Q.   A man owed me $5,500 and couldn't pay. I agreed to take a $10,000 real estate note as payment in full. Do I have to claim the whole amount?

A.   No. Your cost basis is the $5,500. Just like in the last question, you figure your profit ratio which is $4,500 divided by the contract amount of $10,000 = .45 or 45 percent. Forty-five percent of each principal payment would be considered profit.

Q.   What if I sell my personal residence on an installment sale basis?

A.   Selling on contract is only one of the tax advantages private home owners have. Sit down with a good tax consultant and go over all of your possibilities.

Q.   If my buyer doesn't assume my loans and the amount of equity between my receivables and my payables is growing, will I have to pay taxes on the growth?

A.   No. You claim profits according to the computation. Your equity growth has nothing to do with this.

Q.   Do I have to use the installment sale method if I sell on contract?

A.   No. But for some people (dealers) the formulas are different.

Q.   When would it be advisable to claim the whole amount in the year of the sale?

A.   This is hard to answer. I want to say never, but I guess there could be a situation for someone, somewhere to claim it all. I've never seen anyone wanting to do it, once they understood the ramifications. Let me explain. Suppose you had a modest income one year and decided to claim it all right then. Let's look at some things that are pertinent:

(1) What would it be like if you only claimed part of your profits received on installments? (In our first

example you would be claiming $1,800—if short term —instead of $15,000). Could you get refunds (minimize the tax due in other years) with other tax strategies?

(2) When you claim your profit five, ten, and fifteen years down the road, you'll be paying your taxes with inflated dollars.

(3) What happens if you have to foreclose on your buyer a few years from now? You've already claimed your profit so now you'll have to back up, figure the new value basis, etc., and do a nice song and dance routine to get your money back.

CONCLUSION

Q. How can I benefit from this way of claiming my profit?

A. There are several answers to this, but they all center on controlling your money. Computing taxes this way and spreading the liability over a number of years, instead of over one, allows you to turn large quantities of property by keeping more money to invest. The installment sale method lets an investor be just that —an investor—and not have to feel like he is working for the IRS.

EXAMPLES

Form 6252	**Installment Sale Income**	OMB No. 1545-0228
Department of the Treasury Internal Revenue Service	▶ See separate instructions. ▶ Attach to your tax return. ▶ Use a separate form for each sale or other disposition of property on the installment method.	Attachment Sequence No. **79**
Name(s) shown on return		Identifying number 123-45-6789

1	Description of property ▶ Single Family Residence..............		
2a	Date acquired (month, day, year) ▶ 1 / 10 / 80 **b** Date sold (month, day, year) ▶ 1 / 25 / 80		
3	Was the property sold to a related party after May 14, 1980? See instructions	☐ Yes ☒ No	
4	If the answer to question 3 is "Yes," was the property a marketable security? If "Yes," complete Part III. If "No," complete Part III for the year of sale and for 2 years after the year of sale.	☐ Yes ☐ No	

Part I   **Gross Profit and Contract Price.** Complete this part for the year of sale only.

5	Selling price including mortgages and other debts. Do not include interest whether stated or unstated	**5**	50,000 00
6	Mortgages and other debts the buyer assumed or took the property subject to, but not new mortgages the buyer got from a bank or other source . **6** 0		
7	Subtract line 6 from line 5 . . . . **7** 50,000 00		
8	Cost or other basis of property sold **8** 33,000 00		
9	Depreciation allowed or allowable **9** 0		
10	Adjusted basis. Subtract line 9 from line 8 . . . . . **10** 33,000 00		
11	Commissions and other expenses of sale. **11** 2,000 00		
12	Income recapture from Form 4797, Part III. See instructions . . **12**		
13	Add lines 10, 11, and 12	**13**	35,000 00
14	Subtract line 13 from line 5. If zero or less, **stop here.** Do not complete the rest of this form .	**14**	15,000 00
15	If the property described on line 1 above was your main home, enter the total of lines 14 and 22 from Form 2119. Otherwise, enter -0-.	**15**	0
16	**Gross profit.** Subtract line 15 from line 14	**16**	15,000 00
17	Subtract line 13 from line 6. If zero or less, enter -0-.	**17**	0
18	**Contract price.** Add line 7 and line 17	**18**	50,000 00

Part II   **Installment Sale Income.** Complete this part for the year of sale and any year you receive a payment or
have certain debts you must treat as a payment on installment obligations.

19	Gross profit percentage. Divide line 16 by line 18. For years after the year of sale, see instructions	**19**	.3
20	**For year of sale only**—Enter amount from line 17 above; otherwise, enter -0-	**20**	0
21	Payments received during year. See instructions. Do not include interest whether stated or unstated	**21**	6,000 00
22	Add lines 20 and 21	**22**	6,000 00
23	Payments received in prior years. See instructions. Do not include interest whether stated or unstated **23** 0		
24	**Installment sale income.** Multiply line 22 by line 19	**24**	1,800 00
25	Part of line 24 that is ordinary income under recapture rules. See instructions	**25**	0
26	Subtract line 25 from line 24. Enter here and on Schedule D or Form 4797. See instructions .	**26**	1,800 00

Part III   **Related Party Installment Sale Income.** Do not complete if you received the final payment this tax year.

27	Name, address, and taxpayer identifying number of related party ....
28	Did the related party, during this tax year, resell or dispose of the property ("second disposition")? . . . ☐ Yes ☐ No
29	If the answer to question 28 is "Yes," complete lines 30 through 37 below unless one of the following conditions is met. Check only the box that applies

Example 10-1

In this example, a home was purchased for $30,000. $3,000 was put into it as capital improvements. When it was sold, the selling expenses totaled $2,000. The profit is $15,000, but all that will have to be claimed this year is 30 percent of the $6,000 ($5,000 down payment plus $1,000, which is the principal part of the monthly payments). This totals $1,800 (or $720 if this property were held over six months).

Form **6252**	**Installment Sale Income**	OMB No. 1545-0228
Department of the Treasury Internal Revenue Service	▶ See separate instructions.　▶ Attach to your tax return. ▶ Use a separate form for each sale or other disposition of property on the installment method.	Attachment Sequence No. **79**

Name(s) shown on return　　　　　　　　　　　　　　　　　　　　　　Identifying number
123-45-6789

1 Description of property ▶ Single Family Residence

2a Date acquired (month, day, year) ▶ ____/____/____　**b** Date sold (month, day, year) ▶ ____/____/____

3 Was the property sold to a related party after May 14, 1980? See instructions . . . . ☐ Yes　☐ No

4 If the answer to question 3 is "Yes," was the property a marketable security? If "Yes," complete Part III. If
"No," complete Part III for the year of sale and for 2 years after the year of sale. . . . . ☐ Yes　☐ No

Part I **Gross Profit and Contract Price.** Complete this part for the year of sale only.

5	Selling price including mortgages and other debts. Do not include interest whether stated or unstated	**5**
6	Mortgages and other debts the buyer assumed or took the property subject to, but not new mortgages the buyer got from a bank or other source .	**6**
7	Subtract line 6 from line 5	**7**
8	Cost or other basis of property sold	**8**
9	Depreciation allowed or allowable	**9**
10	Adjusted basis. Subtract line 9 from line 8	**10**
11	Commissions and other expenses of sale	**11**
12	Income recapture from Form 4797, Part III. See instructions . .	**12**
13	Add lines 10, 11, and 12	**13**
14	Subtract line 13 from line 5. If zero or less, **stop here.** Do not complete the rest of this form .	**14**
15	If the property described on line 1 above was your main home, enter the total of lines 14 and 22 from Form 2119. Otherwise, enter -0-	**15**
16	**Gross profit.** Subtract line 15 from line 14	**16**
17	Subtract line 13 from line 6. If zero or less, enter -0-	**17**
18	**Contract price.** Add line 7 and line 17	**18**

Part II **Installment Sale Income.** Complete this part for the year of sale and any year you receive a payment or
have certain debts you must treat as a payment on installment obligations.

19	Gross profit percentage. Divide line 16 by line 18. For years after the year of sale, see instructions	**19**	.3
20	**For year of sale only**—Enter amount from line 17 above; otherwise, enter -0-	**20**	
21	Payments received during year. See instructions. Do not include interest whether stated or unstated	**21**	1,200 00
22	Add lines 20 and 21	**22**	1,200 00
23	Payments received in prior years. See instructions. Do not include interest whether stated or unstated . . . . First filed in 1980	**23**	1,800 00
24	**Installment sale income.** Multiply line 22 by line 19	**24**	400 00
25	Part of line 24 that is ordinary income under recapture rules. See instructions	**25**	0
26	Subtract line 25 from line 24. Enter here and on Schedule D or Form 4797. See instructions .	**26**	400 00

Part III **Related Party Installment Sale Income.** Do not complete if you received the final payment this tax year.

27 Name, address, and taxpayer identifying number of related party

28 Did the related party, during this tax year, resell or dispose of the property ("second disposition")? . . . ☐ Yes　☐ No

29 If the answer to question 28 is "Yes," complete lines 30 through 37 below unless one of the following conditions is
met. Check only the box that applies.

Example 10-2

This example shows what will have to be claimed the second year of the sale explained in Example 10-1. Note that the 30 percent (.3) stays the same.

Form **6252**	**Installment Sale Income**	OMB No. 1545-0228
Department of the Treasury Internal Revenue Service	▶ See separate instructions. ▶ Attach to your tax return. ▶ Use a separate form for each sale or other disposition of property on the installment method.	Attachment Sequence No. **79**
Name(s) shown on return		Identifying number **123-45-6789**

1 Description of property ▶ Single Family Residence ....

2a Date acquired (month, day, year) ▶ |_____/_____/_____| b Date sold (month, day, year) ▶ |_____/_____/_____|

3 Was the property sold to a related party after May 14, 1980? See instructions . . . . ☐ Yes ☐ No

4 If the answer to question 3 is "Yes," was the property a marketable security? If "Yes," complete Part III. If "No," complete Part III for the year of sale and for 2 years after the year of sale. . . . . ☐ Yes ☐ No

Part I **Gross Profit and Contract Price.** Complete this part for the year of sale only.

5	Selling price including mortgages and other debts. Do not include interest whether stated or unstated	**5**	
6	Mortgages and other debts the buyer assumed or took the property subject to, but not new mortgages the buyer got from a bank or other source	**6**	
7	Subtract line 6 from line 5 .	**7**	
8	Cost or other basis of property sold	**8**	
9	Depreciation allowed or allowable	**9**	
10	Adjusted basis. Subtract line 9 from line 8	**10**	
11	Commissions and other expenses of sale. . .	**11**	
12	Income recapture from Form 4797, Part III. See instructions	**12**	
13	Add lines 10, 11, and 12	**13**	
14	Subtract line 13 from line 5. If zero or less, **stop here.** Do not complete the rest of this form .	**14**	
15	If the property described on line 1 above was your main home, enter the total of lines 14 and 22 from Form 2119. Otherwise, enter -0-	**15**	
16	**Gross profit.** Subtract line 15 from line 14	**16**	
17	Subtract line 13 from line 6. If zero or less, enter -0- .	**17**	
18	**Contract price.** Add line 7 and line 17	**18**	

Part II **Installment Sale Income.** Complete this part for the year of sale and any year you receive a payment or have certain debts you must treat as a payment on installment obligations.

19	Gross profit percentage. Divide line 16 by line 18. For years after the year of sale, see instructions	**19**	.3
20	**For year of sale only**—Enter amount from line 17 above; otherwise, enter -0- .	**20**	
21	Payments received during year. See instructions. Do not include interest whether stated or unstated	**21**	4,200 00
22	Add lines 20 and 21	**22**	4,200 00
23	Payments received in prior years. See instructions. Do not include interest whether stated or unstated . . . . First filed in 1980 **23**	38,000 00		
24	**Installment sale income.** Multiply line 22 by line 19	**24**	1,260 00
25	Part of line 24 that is ordinary income under recapture rules. See instructions	**25**	0
26	Subtract line 25 from line 24. Enter here and on Schedule D or Form 4797. See instructions	**26**	1,260 00

Part III **Related Party Installment Sale Income.** Do not complete if you received the final payment this tax year.

27 Name, address, and taxpayer identifying number of related party ....

28 Did the related party, during this tax year, resell or dispose of the property ("second disposition")? . . . ☐ Yes ☐ No

29 **If the answer to question 28 is "Yes," complete lines 30 through 37 below unless one of the following conditions is**

Example 10-3

After several years, the ratio stays the same and even then only a small portion would have to be claimed.

Form **6252**

Department of the Treasury
Internal Revenue Service

Installment Sale Income

► See separate instructions. ► Attach to your tax return.
► Use a separate form for each sale or other disposition of property on the installment method.

OMB No. 1545-0228

Attachment
Sequence No. **79**

Name(s) shown on return	Identifying number
	123-45-6789

1 Description of property ► Single Family Residence

2a Date acquired (month, day, year) ► 3 / 12 / 80 b Date sold (month, day, year) ► 4 / 05 / 80

3 Was the property sold to a related party after May 14, 1980? See instructions . . . . ☐ Yes ☒ No

4 If the answer to question 3 is "Yes," was the property a marketable security? If "Yes," complete Part III. If "No," complete Part III for the year of sale and for 2 years after the year of sale. . . . . ☐ Yes ☐ No

Part I   Gross Profit and Contract Price. Complete this part for the year of sale only.

5	Selling price including mortgages and other debts. Do not include interest whether stated or unstated	5	50,000 00
6	Mortgages and other debts the buyer assumed or took the property subject to, but not new mortgages the buyer got from a bank or other source .	6	36,000 00
7	Subtract line 6 from line 5	7	14,000 00
8	Cost or other basis of property sold	8	33,000 00
9	Depreciation allowed or allowable	9	0
10	Adjusted basis. Subtract line 9 from line 8	10	33,000 00
11	Commissions and other expenses of sale.	11	2,000 00
12	Income recapture from Form 4797, Part III. See instructions . .	12	
13	Add lines 10, 11, and 12	13	35,000 00
14	Subtract line 13 from line 5. If zero or less, **stop here.** Do not complete the rest of this form .	14	15,000 00
15	If the property described on line 1 above was your main home, enter the total of lines 14 and 22 from Form 2119. Otherwise, enter -0-.	15	0
16	**Gross profit.** Subtract line 15 from line 14	16	15,000 00
17	Subtract line 13 from line 6. If zero or less, enter -0-	17	1,000 00
18	**Contract price.** Add line 7 and line 17	18	15,000 00

Part II   Installment Sale Income. Complete this part for the year of sale and any year you receive a payment or have certain debts you must treat as a payment on installment obligations.

19	Gross profit percentage. Divide line 16 by line 18. For years after the year of sale, see instructions	19	100%
20	**For year of sale only**—Enter amount from line 17 above; otherwise, enter -0-	20	1,000 00
21	Payments received during year. See instructions. Do not include interest whether stated or unstated	21	5,200 00
22	Add lines 20 and 21	22	6,200 00
23	Payments received in prior years. See instructions. Do not include interest whether stated or unstated	23	0	
24	**Installment sale income.** Multiply line 22 by line 19	24	6,200 00
25	Part of line 24 that is ordinary income under recapture rules. See instructions	25	0
26	Subtract line 25 from line 24. Enter here and on Schedule D or Form 4797. See instructions .	26	6,200 00

Part III   Related Party Installment Sale Income. Do not complete if you received the final payment this tax year.

27 Name, address, and taxpayer identifying number of related party

28 Did the related party, during this tax year, resell or dispose of the property ("second disposition")? . . . ☐ Yes ☐ No

29 **If the answer to question 28 is "Yes," complete lines 30 through 37 below unless one of the following conditions is** met. Check only the box that applies

Example 10-4

This $6,200 might seem high but we did only put $3,000 into the property. The $5,000 down payment that we received was enough to cover selling expenses of $2,000. When we refinanced the property, we freed this $3,000 plus $3,000 more. The results are $6,000 cash in our pocket; we have an equity contract of $9,000—netting $90 a month; and all we have to claim is $6,200 (which can be offset by other deductions).

Form **6252**	**Installment Sale Income**	OMB No. 1545-0228
Department of the Treasury Internal Revenue Service	▶ See separate instructions. ▶ Attach to your tax return. ▶ Use a separate form for each sale or other disposition of property on the installment method.	Attachment Sequence No. **79**
Name(s) shown on return		Identifying number 123-45-6789

1	Description of property ▶ ......Duplex......			
2a	Date acquired (month, day, year) ▶ ⌊ 3 / 13 / 81 ⌋ **b** Date sold (month, day, year) ▶ ⌊ 4 / 5 /81 ⌋			
3	Was the property sold to a related party after May 14, 1980? See instructions . . . . ☐ Yes ☒ No			
4	If the answer to question 3 is "Yes," was the property a marketable security? If "Yes," complete Part III. If "No," complete Part III for the year of sale and for 2 years after the year of sale. . . . . ☐ Yes ☐ No			

Part I **Gross Profit and Contract Price.** Complete this part for the year of sale only.

5	Selling price including mortgages and other debts. Do not include interest whether stated or unstated		**5**	50,000 00
6	Mortgages and other debts the buyer assumed or took the property subject to, but not new mortgages the buyer got from a bank or other source .	**6** 36,000 00		
7	Subtract line 6 from line 5	**7** 14,000 00		
8	Cost or other basis of property sold	**8** 37,000 00		
9	Depreciation allowed or allowable	**9** 0		
10	Adjusted basis. Subtract line 9 from line 8	**10** 37,000 00		
11	Commissions and other expenses of sale	**11** 2,000 00		
12	Income recapture from Form 4797, Part III. See instructions . .	**12**		
13	Add lines 10, 11, and 12		**13**	39,000 00
14	Subtract line 13 from line 5. If zero or less, **stop here.** Do not complete the rest of this form .		**14**	11,000 00
15	If the property described on line 1 above was your main home, enter the total of lines 14 and 22 from Form 2119. Otherwise, enter -0-		**15**	0
16	**Gross profit.** Subtract line 15 from line 14		**16**	11,000 00
17	Subtract line 13 from line 6. If zero or less, enter -0-		**17**	0
18	**Contract price.** Add line 7 and line 17		**18**	50,000 00

Part II **Installment Sale Income.** Complete this part for the year of sale and any year you receive a payment or have certain debts you must treat as a payment on installment obligations.

19	Gross profit percentage. Divide line 16 by line 18. For years after the year of sale, see instructions		**19**	.22
20	**For year of sale only**—Enter amount from line 17 above; otherwise, enter -0-		**20**	0
21	Payments received during year. See instructions. Do not include interest whether stated or unstated		**21**	5,200 00
22	Add lines 20 and 21		**22**	5,200 00
23	Payments received in prior years. See instructions. Do not include interest whether stated or unstated	**23** 0		
24	**Installment sale income.** Multiply line 22 by line 19		**24**	1,144 00
25	Part of line 24 that is ordinary income under recapture rules. See instructions		**25**	0
26	Subtract line 25 from line 24. Enter here and on Schedule D or Form 4797. See instructions .		**26**	1,144 00

Part III **Related Party Installment Sale Income.** Do not complete if you received the final payment this tax year.

27	Name, address, and taxpayer identifying number of related party ....
28	Did the related party, during this tax year, resell or dispose of the property ("second disposition")? . . . ☐ Yes ☐ No
29	**If the answer to question 28 is "Yes," complete lines 30 through 37 below unless one of the following conditions is** met. Check only the box that applies

Example 10-5

In this example, the underlying mortgage was assumed by the buyer, but the amount assumed is lower than the cost basis. Only amounts actually received would have to be claimed.

Form **6252**	**Installment Sale Income**	OMB No. 1545-0228
Department of the Treasury Internal Revenue Service	▶ **See separate instructions.** ▶ **Attach to your tax return.** ▶ **Use a separate form for each sale or other disposition of property on the installment method.**	Attachment Sequence No. **79**
Name(s) shown on return		Identifying number 123-45-6789

1	Description of property ▶ Single Family Residence			
2a	Date acquired (month, day, year) ▶ / / **b** Date sold (month, day, year) ▶ / /			
3	Was the property sold to a related party after May 14, 1980? See instructions	☐ Yes	☐ No
4	If the answer to question 3 is "Yes," was the property a marketable security? If "Yes," complete Part III. If "No," complete Part III for the year of sale and for 2 years after the year of sale.	☐ Yes	☐ No

Part I   **Gross Profit and Contract Price.** Complete this part for the year of sale only.

5	Selling price including mortgages and other debts. Do not include interest whether stated or unstated	**5**	50,000	00
6	Mortgages and other debts the buyer assumed or took the property subject to, but not new mortgages the buyer got from a bank or other source .	**6**	0	
7	Subtract line 6 from line 5	**7**	50,000	00
8	Cost or other basis of property sold	**8**	33,000	00
9	Depreciation allowed or allowable	**9**	0	
10	Adjusted basis. Subtract line 9 from line 8	**10**	33,000	00
11	Commissions and other expenses of sale	**11**	2,000	00
12	Income recapture from Form 4797, Part III. See instructions . .	**12**		
13	Add lines 10, 11, and 12	**13**	35,000	00
14	Subtract line 13 from line 5. If zero or less, **stop here.** Do not complete the rest of this form .	**14**	15,000	00
15	If the property described on line 1 above was your main home, enter the total of lines 14 and 22 from Form 2119. Otherwise, enter -0-	**15**	0	
16	**Gross profit.** Subtract line 15 from line 14	**16**	15,000	00
17	Subtract line 13 from line 6. If zero or less, enter -0-	**17**	0	
18	**Contract price.** Add line 7 and line 17	**18**	50,000	00

Part II   **Installment Sale Income.** Complete this part for the year of sale and any year you receive a payment or
have certain debts you must treat as a payment on installment obligations.

19	Gross profit percentage. Divide line 16 by line 18. For years after the year of sale, see instructions	**19**	.3	
20	**For year of sale only**—Enter amount from line 17 above; otherwise, enter -0-	**20**	0	
21	Payments received during year. See instructions. Do not include interest whether stated or unstated	**21**	16,800	00
22	Add lines 20 and 21	**22**	16,800	00
23	Payments received in prior years. See instructions. Do not include interest whether stated or unstated	**23**	0	
24	**Installment sale income.** Multiply line 22 by line 19	**24**	5,040	00
25	Part of line 24 that is ordinary income under recapture rules. See instructions . . .	**25**	0	
26	Subtract line 25 from line 24. Enter here and on Schedule D or Form 4797. See instructions .	**26**	5,040	00

Part III   **Related Party Installment Sale Income.** Do not complete if you received the final payment this tax year.

27	Name, address, and taxpayer identifying number of related party	
28	Did the related party, during this tax year, resell or dispose of the property ("second disposition")? . . . ☐ Yes ☐ No	
29	**If the answer to question 28 is "Yes," complete lines 30 through 37 below unless one of the following conditions is** met. Check only the box that applies	

Example 10-6

In this example, $8,000 was invested, but the $16,000 down payment received more than returned the $8,000, plus an additional $8,000 was received.

A $7,000 equity contract was created—netting $70 a month. All that has to be claimed is $5,040.

CHAPTER **11**

Why the Concept Works—
A List of Reasons

1. It gets the beginning investor making money now.
2. It creates steady, reliable monthly income.
3. The problem of burying down payments is alleviated. You get your down payments back each time.
4. All fix-up money is used to create new value that is then capitalized on.
5. All closing costs can be returned—if done right.
6. The wraparound loan and the underlying loans are definite numbers—good for any financial statement.
7. Foreclosures can be purchased (usually requiring some cash) and then sold to immediately generate larger profits.
8. Any good idea in real estate can be used to enhance the machine's effectiveness.
9. The concept stresses value now, instead of later.
10. Each property becomes the springboard for the next property. Compare this to constantly looking for sources of money if the property is held as a rental.
11. Cashing out does not create a larger tax problem.
12. Taxes are spread out due to the installment sales treatment. Profits are claimed as they are received.

13. Most interest income is offset by interest expense, generating small tax consequences.
14. Assets can be quickly created to build up a financial statement for further investment.
15. The foreclosure rate is almost nil. People are better at making house payments than paying rent.
16. Property owners take better care of their homes than renters do.
17. The notes can be discounted and sold for cash.
18. These notes are created from scratch. If the process is done right, the cost of creating a note is zero.
19. Time problems, which are so prevalent with rentals, are almost totally eliminated.
20. If cash is needed, and a person doesn't want to sell, the notes can be used for collateral.
21. Most people need more income to invest in other things. This can be done quickly.
22. It is easier to buy when you know you can sell for a little higher payment (than rents).
23. Banks with all their attendant problems are avoided.
24. Eventually the buyer will sell or seek new financing and cash out your equity.
25. If the $10,000 equity is netting $100 per month, and you then receive all of your $10,000 equity, the $10,000 cash could buy a $20,000 note netting around $200 per month.
26. Payment service organizations can be employed, for a small fee, to take care of receiving and making your monthly payments.
27. Once properties sell, figuring out the tax forms is easy.
28. The wraparound pay-off period is longer than that for underlying loans. Once paid off, the outgoing payments also stop, netting more monthly income.
29. Many houses can be sold as fixer-uppers, but they cannot be rented as fixer-uppers. This helps, because not a lot of cash is needed.

30. Banks understand profits; they have a hard time with losses (either actual or on paper) created by rental properties.

31. If something were to happen to you, you have good assets for disability retirement or for your family that do not require being a landlord.

32. The cash flow gives you freedom to learn and grow. While necessity is the mother of invention, a leisurely stroll is a good catalyst for ideas.

33. You won't get discouraged by collecting rent and having tenants who beat up the place and then don't pay their rent.

34. If you must foreclose, you can get the property back and resell at an increased value.

35. If you take the property back, you can keep any money put in by the buyer.

36. If you have rentals (and even if you have a positive income), you can't quit being a landlord. It is almost impossible to wind down.

37. With notes receivable, collection is easy. If you have rentals, it is difficult to find a good property manager.

38. Many investors with large incomes should be passive investors. This note income (with passive attributes) is just the ticket to purchase other tax-sheltered passive investments.

39. It is time-tested. People have been selling property like this for years.

40. You can sell the property quickly this way.

41. Because you are doing the qualifying (not the banks), you have many potential buyers.

42. If you're willing to carry the financing, you can increase the price and some of the terms a little.

43. Duplication breeds success. Put your money in, get it out; create a note, then repeat it again and again.

44. Purchasing with a low down payment, then selling with a higher down, redoubles money-making efforts.

45. Once a property is money machined, it doesn't get sick, as people can.

46. It is fun and it works.

47. By keeping you busy in the real estate arena, it helps you find other good deals.

48. If the property is held for over six months and then sold, the investment qualifies for long-term capital gains treatment, an additional tax break.

49. Usually the underlying loans amortize at a faster rate than the wraparound loan, thus the equity (the difference between the receivable and the payable) grows each time a payment is made.

50. Each note can be traded for other properties.

51. A note can be used as security for a pledge to do something (a form of collateral).

52. You'll learn how to buy and sell notes, mortgages, or deeds of trust.

53. You learn how to read title reports to help determine value and marketability.

54. Measuring the effectiveness of your investments is a must. You'll learn all about yields and what your money is doing.

55. Your financial statements start looking good. Why? Because there is no guesswork in your numbers.

56. You can do it in various cities if you move around. It's very difficult to have rentals in different cities.

57. You'll get and stay excited because of the mental freedom knowing money will always be there.

58. You can do it part-time and quit anytime you want.

59. Eventually, you will do a money machine with most of your rental properties anyway. Why not start now and get good at it?

60. This plan allows you to concentrate all your efforts on just one idea and thereby makes success easier.

61. The process teaches you to become so active at finding good deals that if a proper rental property is found, it can be kept for the tax write-offs.

CHAPTER **12**

More Information on Contracts

Before we get into the particulars of what contracts can be used for, let's cover the two types of contracts. (Once again contracts mean mortgages, trust deeds, real estate contracts and other notes).

The first type of contract is created by taking one's equity in a piece of property on installments. All underlying mortgages, if any, are assumed by the buyer. It only has payments coming in or a promise to pay at some future date. For this definition, it doesn't matter whether it's in first, second, third, or whatever position on the property.

The second type of equity contract is that equity which represents the difference between a receivable contract and a payable contract. Some refer to it as a "wraparound" mortgage. But I prefer to call it an "over-riding" contract or mortgage, in contrast to an "underlying" loan. Over-riding loans take the premise that the buyer does not assume the underlying loans; the seller maintains all underlying responsibilities.

The difference between the over-riding loan and the underlying loan varies, creating an increase, a decrease, or no change at all (which is hard to do). It is mandatory to understand this principle before buying or selling on install-ments. Look at the following examples for a further explanation.

Example 1: Equity Increase

$60,000 receivable @ $600 per month ($540 interest / $60 principal).

$40,000 payable @ $400 per month ($320 interest / $80 principal).

A $20 equity increase results because $20 more is going off the underlying loan than is coming off the over-riding loan. All contracts should be set up like this so that the underlying loans pay off before the over-riding loan, at which time there will be assets but no liabilities.

Example 2: Equity Decrease

$60,000 receivable @ $600 per month ($520 interest / $80 principal).

$40,000 payable @ $400 per month ($360 interest / $40 principal).

A $40 equity decrease results from $40 more coming off the over-riding loan than is going off the underlying loan.

It would be easy to think that the only adjustment to influence the amount applied to principal would be to raise or lower the monthly payment, but you could also raise or lower the interest rate. If the interest rate was lower on the over-riding loan, then more would come off as principal payment. If too much is applied to the principal, then it will cause your equity to decrease.

There is one other way to influence how much of the payment will be interest and how much will be principal, and that is to raise or lower the purchase price. I suggest not altering the purchase price. Alter the interest rate and/or the monthly payment.

Example 3: Equity Stays the Same

In order for this to happen, there would have to be a great amount of manipulation on somebody's part. The chances of it happening are rare, but if it does happen, it won't stay that way. Even if both amounts applied to the principal were the same this month, they would change the next month, due to the difference in the total balance.

Of these three types of equity situations, Example 1 is best and Example 3 is nearly impossible. Because Example 2 is unfavorable, it needs to have some further explanation and some possible remedies.

In an equity decreasing situation there is a risk that the over-riding loan will catch up to and pass the underlying loan (especially in loans with small equity splits, i.e. a $95,000 receivable and $90,000 payable). This would be a very awkward situation. Think about it. You would not only have a negative equity growth, which is bad enough (every month your net worth would decrease and look bad on your financial statement), but also the deed you would be required to give your buyer (for satisfaction of mortgage), would be due before you received your deed.

If a mistake is made and you find yourself in this position (maybe you assumed a loan that had a negative equity growth with the loan underlying it), there are two remedies. First, you could renegotiate one of the mortgages and re-record it. Second, and this is probably the easiest way, you could exercise the payment clause that contains the words "or more" and make a larger payment on the underlying loan. The additional amount would be applied to principal. Make sure this extra payment is large enough to set it straight. This does not have to be done each month. It can be done when you deem appropriate. For example, you might have an $80,000 receivable with a $40,000 payable. The negative equity growth could be $40 a month, and even though the $80,000 is paying off faster it will probably be down to a $30,000 receivable when the $40,000 hits zero. It was moving up, but did not catch it.

WHAT CAN BE DONE WITH CONTRACTS?

Many things can be done with equity contracts. The following lists give some good ideas, and in the wonderful world of investing money, more could be developed. Here are a few:

1. Hang onto them and live by the conditions of the mortgage and you will eventually be paid off in one of two ways:

    A. The contract will run the distance.
    B. The purchaser will come up with the money (i.e. refinance) and pay off the balance owing.

2. You will have to foreclose if the buyer doesn't pay. In this case you could either get the house back or have your loan taken over by the next person down the chain of title. Foreclosure laws vary greatly from state to state. If you are confronted with this, obtain good legal help.

3. You can borrow against your equities. Some banks and many people will use contracts as collateral. The value put on a contract will usually be at about 50 percent of its face value. This is a great advantage because you don't have to pay taxes on this borrowed amount. It's a good way to move on to bigger and better things without paying taxes.

4. You can pledge these contracts as security for performance. For example, I wanted to buy a five-plex unit, but the man wanted $5,000 down and I only had $2,000 to give him. I promised to pay the other $3,000 in two years. I gave him an assignment for collateral purposes only, on a $7,000 equity contract which I held. I got the best of both worlds. I was able to put very little down and tie up both units, AND I was able to continue receiving the payments from the contract.

5. You can sell your contract equities. This is frequently done, so let's go over some things people look for in buying contracts.

The first and most important thing is the yield (or how fast they are going to get their money back). The formula is simple for calculating a simple yield (the true yield is slightly different).

Rate of Return = Net received (cash returned) for one year divided by the amount invested.

For example, if you purchased a $10,000 contract with $100 monthly payments for $5,000, your rate of return would be:

$$\frac{\$1,200 \ (\$100 \ X \ 12 \ months)}{\$5,000} = 24\% \ yield$$

Paying $6,000 for that contract would be:

$$\frac{\$1,200}{\$6,000} = 20\% \ yield$$

Other aspects of figuring yields to consider:
1. The return in subsequent years is different because:
   A. The payments might change.
   B. Some of the cash invested has returned, so the yield should be refigured.
   C. Equity growth can be added as part of the yield, but will only be received later as a bonus, when the contract pays off.
2. Balloon payments drastically change the nature of purchasing a contract, but unless received the first year, they should not be figured in the first year's yield.
3. Anyone buying and selling contracts figures yields to determine what he will give or take for the contracts. It is not, however, the only consideration. Even if it were, there are so many variables that it becomes subjective. Everyone puts values on different as-

pects. One company might figure the first year rate of return and base all of its decision on that. Another might figure pay-off time, especially balloons. Still another might only be interested in interest rates on the loans.

Finally, it comes down to the old axiom, "It's worth what somebody will pay for it."

The second thing is the value of the property, and, more specifically, the position the contract has in the value structure of the property. For example: If the property is worth $50,000 and the $10,000 equity contract you have for sale represents the amount between a $48,000 receivable and a $38,000 payable, it will be hard to sell. But on this same property, if the equity represents the difference between a $30,000 receivable and a $20,000 payable, it will draw a better price because there's plenty of protection left between the $50,000 and the $30,000.

The third thing that's important is where the property stands in the chain of title. Like the last point, protection is the main concern. Someone buying a contract wants to make sure he's getting the equity position he thinks he is getting. Understanding a title report and getting title insurance will alleviate this problem. Generally speaking, people who buy a contract would rather buy an equity between a receivable and a payable. This way they have equity growth and control the underlying payments—making sure that these loans get paid.

PAPER TIGERS

The following is from a special report I wrote to accompany my home study course on buying, selling and using deep discounted mortgages, deeds of trust, and contracts. See the back of the book for information about this all-day seminar entitled Paper Tigers.

There are many good investments in the world today, but few stand out as practical in producing cash flow for the long term from short term efforts and money. But deep- discounted second mortgages clearly produce remarkable results. That's what this report is about—hassle-free cash flow.

First, when we talk about second mortgages, we mean Trust Deeds, Real Estate Contracts, Agreements for Sale, Mortgages, etc. Different states use different names, but whatever name is used, the "paper" or document is a recorded lien (encumbrance) against real property. They usually have monthly payments wherein a certain amount goes to interest and some to principal reduction to pay off the mortgage. We will use the term mortgage here often to refer generically refer to this type of debt.

Many people wonder how "paper" or "contracts" are created. It's really quite simple. When someone sells a property he can receive cash (usually from the buyer's down payment and new loan) or he can "take back" or "carry" the financing himself. Usually it is a combination of both.

For example: A house is sold for $100,000. The buyer only has $18,000. He could get a new loan for $80,000, maybe, but in this case there is a $60,000 existing first mortgage which is assumable. The payment is $600. The seller—wanting to (a) avoid taxes, (b) sell quickly, (c) create monthly income, or (d) any other purpose—agrees to carry back a second mortgage for the remaining $22,000. He agrees to 11% interest with payment of $300 per month. This loan will run about 20 years.

Now before we move on to buying the mortgage, let's explore one other possibility. The seller could take the $18,000 down payment and create a "wraparound" mortgage with the buyer. People somehow want to make this complicated, but it's really quite simple. A document is drawn up stating the buyer owes the seller $82,000 ($100,000 purchase price minus the $18,000 down payment). The seller keeps the first mortgage in his name and continues making payment on it. The interest on the new loan of $82,000 is once again set up at 11%. The payment is set at $900. This mortgage will take about 25 years to pay off. The good part for the seller (and for us if we buy this mortgage) is the "spread" between the two loans. The bottom loan has a lower interest rate, therefore it is paying off faster - say 22 years.

Let's look at a few points that don't readily meet the eye:

1.   Because there is a difference between the principal amount of the two loans, the mortgage holder is actually increasing his equity with each monthly payment. This is very important.

Back to our example so you can see how this works. On our $600 payment on this first mortgage, let's say about $60 is principal and $540 is interest. On our "wrap" the principal portion of the $900 payment is only $40. The rest is interest. This means our liability is paying off faster than our asset. In fact, we're increasing our net worth by $20 each month.

2.   This means after many years the bottom mortgage will be paid off and there will still be money coming in on the "wrap" mortgage.

Please note: There is equity growth between the notes only for as long as both exist. When the bottom loan pays off there is no more growth, as there is no difference. At this time the "wrap" mortgage just pays off. Later you'll see why these types of loans are the type you want to keep.

Back to the general transaction: Whichever way the property is sold, the seller has created a $22,000 equity position. He is netting $300 per month. One last point: This is equity which the seller didn't actually earn. It came about from buying this property and letting inflation do its thing.

Now a few years have passed. For some unknown reason, the seller needs more cash. It's Christmas, the kids need college tuition, he's out of work or a hundred other reasons, but whatever, he's willing to take a lump sum and let someone buy this mortgage (which really means: buy the full income stream this mortgage produces).

This is where you come in. You can find these deals at 40 to 70 cents on the dollar. For our example, we'll use 50% or 50 cents on the dollar. Is it really possible? Emphatically yes! You can find more in some areas than in others, but they are available.

You find them by:
1. Running a simple ad in the paper.
2. Giving out cards and brochures to everyone explaining what you do.
3. Checking the courthouse records and contacting the private parties who have carried back mortgages.
4. Talking to Real Estate agents for their own notes or notes of clients.
5. Talking to and building relationships with title companies, escrow agents, collection companies, etc.

Finding them is not that difficult. Yes, it takes awhile to get good at it, but soon you'll have so many, you won't be able to buy all of them.

Once you've found a mortgage, tie it up. Sign a commitment of purchase, an option agreement or even an earnest money agreement, but get a commitment. You can get out of the deal with an escape clause like, "This purchase is subject to final inspection and approval of buyer."

Rates of Return

The price you'll agree to depends on the yield (i.e., how much money you'll get back, and how fast). You can figure a real yield with any good calculator. With this you'll take all the remaining payments, enter them, take the interest rate, the amount you'll pay (or the yield you desire) and you'll figure out if it's a good deal. Yields of 14-35% are very common. Let me take time out here and interject my own personal philosophy.

Yields are great. You'll need to get good at figuring them out, but they don't tell the whole story. And if you get too bogged down in numbers, you'll forget to make the really big money. I'm more inclined to deal with a cash-on-cash return (yield) and keep it simple.

For example, if you pay $10,000 for a note with a $200 payment, you will take in $2,400 in one year. That's 24% on your investment. While this is not the true yield, it gets you in the ball park and lets you see how much your money will earn.

One more point. When you figure yields, you take the annual payments back in and calculate a one year yield. But think what you're getting in payments every month. Just putting that money into a savings account will earn even more. And each month it gets better.

Also, once you've done this for awhile, you'll have enough cash flow to start buying more. This really gets fun when you see a group of notes spinning off enough income to buy more. This is called "compounding of assets." Most people have never heard of it.

Restructuring

We're buying these notes for cash flow. Some of them may have graduated payments, thereby increasing our cash flow in the future. Others are prime candidates for what we call "restructuring." Simply put, we're going to try to get the homeowner (payor) on the note to do one of two things. The first would be to get him to agree to a higher payment. Now, why would anyone want to pay more? For one thing, he'll pay off the loan faster and save hundreds or, more likely, thousands of dollars in interest.

We may also add a little "sugar" to the deal. For example, if he'll raise the payment from $600 to $700, we'll lower the interest rate on the mortgage from 11% to 10%. If he can pay $800 we'll drop it to 8%, and so on. Now he really benefits; not only is a lot more going to principal because of the extra principal amount, less is going to interest. Some people have cut mortgage times from 30 years to less than 10 years using this method.

Why would we want to do this? Remember our goal (especially at first) is to recapture our money as fast as possible. Yes, the interest rate is important, but the return of our capital as quickly as possible is paramount.

Refinancing

The other strategies we can take are even better. This one can be accomplished on properties where the people and the property are conducive to refinance. Here's how it works. The homeowner has a situation that may be better for him if he were to refinance at a lower interest rate or obtain a loan with better (lower) payments (like an Adjustable Rate Mortgage).

He may:
1. Have a high interest rate second mortgage.
2. Have high payments on the first or second mortgage.
3. Have a high interest rate first mortgage.
4. Have increasing payments on the first or second mortgage.
5. Have enough equity to refinance and use the money elsewhere.
6. Have a need (other debts and expenditures) for cash to reduce his monthly cash drain.

If he refinances and pays us off, he may be in a lot better position. We can add a few incentives, like paying him $1,000 the day we get paid off. Or we could pay the closing costs (the amount would depend on the profits we're to make).

Let's look at an example: we've spent $12,000 for a $20,000 note. Five weeks from now the owner's new loan pays us off. We agreed to pay $1,000 to him and $1,000 toward the closing costs. We put in $12,000 plus this extra $2,000 totaling $14,000. We net $6,000. Not bad for five weeks and about 3 to 4 hours of work. Note: If we could pay the $12,000 out of the closing we may not have to tie up one cent. If you have the right team, how many of these can you do in one month?

Tax Advantages

When you buy a note, you'll receive your gain over a period of time—on the installment sales method. A portion of each principal payment received represents gain; the other portion is just a return of your cost. The IRS form for this is form 6252. Tax laws change, so seek competent help from **experienced** professionals. Also, note your state laws may deviate from the federal guidelines.

Obviously interest income is a reportable item. Buying, selling, and restructuring notes is not a tax shelter. It provides profits and income. Remember, you are in the cash flow business. Set aside funds accordingly and take other measures to save on taxes.

Risks—virtually everything that can go wrong—can be:
1.   Avoided by checking out the details.
2.   Insured against—both fire and title.
3.   Compensated for in the purchase price.
4.   Remedied with certain strategies designed to solve problems.

Most things that seem like problems can be turned around to help you make more money.

Wraps are good to buy and keep as they also have a slight equity growth between the two mortgages. Remember the bottom loan is paying off faster. This means your financial statement looks better every month so long as there is an underlying loan. As popular as "wraps" have been, however, there just aren't that many of them available.

The economy affects this business to some degree. One concern is interest rates. The good thing is whether they go up or down, we benefit. If interest rates rise, more sellers have to carry back financing so the buyer can afford the payments. This abundance allows for better deals as we can shop around more. When the rates drop, these same people are more likely to refinance to get the lower rates and pay us off.

CHAPTER **13**

Tips on Fixing Up

What Do You Have To Crew About?

One of the most difficult decisions I had to make as a small investor was whether to do the fix-up work myself, use subcontractors, or hire employees. Once I made a decision and thought the problem was solved, something else would always come up.

Let me pose the dilemma. When I first started investing, I took the advice of others and used subcontractors. For most types of buildings, this would have been fine, but remodeling has its own unique problems. Once the subcontractor started a job, invariably he would find something else that needed repairing. On one occasion I had a man putting in a new toilet. Once the old one was out, he could see that the floor was rotting. To do that work meant changing the original bid. Then he found that the joists had termites because of the moisture—another new bid. Now it involved the ceiling of the room below—and another new bid. I felt like a yo-yo.

Another time a subcontractor agreed to paint a room for $80. As he began applying the paint, the old wallpaper began to bubble. It would have taken too long to scrape and re-do the wall so we paneled it. It took three different bids to do this job.

After going through this several times, I decided to hire my own man. Then, if anything was wrong, he would just go ahead and fix it. I soon found, though, that having employees also had its drawbacks. I'm not going to say which is better, but I will list the good and bad points of each. Each house (situation) is different. You'll have to decide.

EMPLOYEES

Good Points:
1.   If you can find good employees, they could relieve a lot of your pressure by running errands between jobs.
2.   They have more time to learn your system and how you like things done.
3.   You can schedule your jobs to fit your time frame and coordinate getting priorities done a lot easier than with independent contractors.
4.   Under your direction, they can watch out for you and get the best prices possible for materials.

Bad Points:
1.   It's your time they're using up. If they break down on the freeway, you'll probably be their taxi service.
2.   Sometimes they'll disregard your priorities, like putting low quality carpeting into a nice home. You'll have to be ready to inspect their work at all times.
3.   You'll have to pay all kinds of taxes and insurance for them. Be prepared to get a good bookkeeper.
4.   Your goals are not the same as theirs. You're trying to get a house livable by Friday and they're looking forward to Friday because it's payday.
5.   If they get sick or leave, the work doesn't get done until they can be replaced.
6.   They may not always be honest. Remember, they are handling YOUR tools and YOUR materials.

SUBCONTRACTORS

Good Points:
1. Generally, they're working by the job so:
   A. They work fast because they don't get paid until it's done.
   B. They do it right the first time.
2. You can get bids and keep the price down.
3. You don't have to worry about taxes and insurance.
4. They are using, losing and abusing their own tools.

Bad Points:
1. They don't always do the quality work they've promised. Sometimes the job has to be done completely over at their expense, but causing you time delays.
2. Once you've paid them some of the money, they might not perform as you'd expect. For example: I needed a house painted. A subcontractor (who was also a friend) gave me a bid of $375 for labor only. I would supply the paint and brushes. I told him that $375 was too low—$450 was a fair price—and I wouldn't mind paying that if he did a nice job by my deadline. He asked when he would get paid. I asked him when he would be finished and he said the following Wednesday. I told him I'd pay him that Wednesday. Wednesday came and he was only about one-third done, but he really needed some money. The ensuing conversation was right out of kindergarten.

   "You told me you'd pay me Wednesday."
   "But you promised to be finished Wednesday."
   "But you promised me the money today, and I need it or the bank will take away my car."
   I paid the money in full with a promise from him that he would complete the job by that Saturday. Six weeks later I had to pay my crew to finish the job. This sort of thing is common.

3.   They're acting in their own best interest.

You see, both ways have advantages as well as disadvantages. There were times when I used only subcontractors and, if I kept on top of them, everything worked out all right. Other times I used only employees and the same thing held true.

In either case, if I could get them to think like me, then what I wanted to happen would happen. But most people aren't used to operating within someone else's time requirements or to someone else's standards.

Lock into Definite Times

I received a bid from a man to paint a few rooms. "When can you be done?" I asked.
"Well, I'll get started tomorrow."
"I appreciate that, but when will you be done?"
"Let me see, it will take me about two days."
"That's fine, but when will you be finished?"
"Why are you so worried about that? I'll get done."
"Because I have to be here at that time to pay you."
"Okay, I'll be done Thursday."
"What time Thursday?"
"3:30."
"Okay, I'll see you Thursday, at 3:30."
Like I said before, it's hard to get people to work in your time plan and commit themselves.

Bids and Counter Bids

A note of caution should be taken when offering a subcontractor less than the bid he has given. I realize that this should be the normal way of doing business, but I have found that once their bid is compromised so is the quality of their work.

It got to the point where I just said yes or no to their bids. I would rather get someone else than have a subcontractor feel slighted and then justified if his work is not up to par.

Once subcontractors know this, the bids they offer are usually fair. I want them happy doing my jobs. Sometimes I carry it to the other extreme and offer them more if their bid is too low. When I do this, I usually get better results and in better time. This is a good place to use the Golden Rule.

DOING THE WORK YOURSELF

Good Points:
1. You save money by controlling material costs and not having to pay someone else.
2. You control the quality of the workmanship.
3. You do the work in your own time to meet your deadlines.

Bad Points:

While you're fixing the toilet and saving $25, you could have used that same time to purchase a house that would make you thousands of dollars. This point alone is why I never do the work myself. It would be better to pay the highest bidder and go out there where the BIG money is.

Let's cover some other aspects of fixing up places.

How Much Work Should I Do?

Remember, the idea is to turn houses. Generally, cosmetic work will raise the value of the house, but I've found that the extra dollars spent trying to improve some houses don't always raise the value much.

For example, a house in a run-down neighborhood will have a top value on it—no matter how much money is put into it. So determine the top value of the home and only fix it up to reach that point. Any more fix-up is a waste of money and

Don't Waste Money

time. Weigh each property. Get in and out with as little work as possible. Let someone else fix it up to be "fit for a king." Once you understand this concept, the proper question might not be, "Should I use subcontractors or employees?" but, "Should I be doing this at all?" Question yourself on each move.

Should You Live in the House?

No. Not as a general practice. If you want to remodel the house you're in, fine, but if you're thinking of moving your family from one house to another—don't. The exception, of course, is, if you find a house you like better than the one you're in, go ahead and move. Remember, though, no one lives well in a dusty mess. I've seen too much hardship brought on families by living in a mess, fixing it up, then moving on to another mess. Keep your business and pleasure separate from one another.

Bathrooms and Kitchens

If you have to fix up, start here. Women usually make the decisions on the house and that's where they look first. Pay attention to color and arrangements.

CONCLUSION

Weigh the following:

1. How much did the acquisition cost?
2. How much more money do you have?
3. Could this money be spent better elsewhere?
4. How much time do you have?
5. What will cleaning it up do to the value? (Many times that's all it takes to make a good profit.)

6.   What is the minimum amount you could put into it to make it "cute?"
7.   Are there other investors or people out there who will buy it "as is?"

Use your team of advisors to help you decide, then move on it and get it ready. And whether you use subcontractors or employees, surround yourself with good people.

CHAPTER **14**

Tips on Selling

Now that you have laid the proper foundation with your purchase arrangements and fixed up your property, it's time to carry through with the third phase of the A.C.E. plan. I must stress, once again, the need to avoid costly entanglements. Have a good picture of what you want out of the house in terms of total price, monthly payments, and interest rates. In order for the house to sell quickly, you might want to make these costs a little lower than average to attract a large number of prospective buyers.

If you have plenty of offers to choose from, the chances of having to sell to someone on cluttered terms is lessened. When you have only a few looky-lous, their terms start to dominate your terms. If this happens, then some sort of unfavorable entanglements will occur.

To have as many people as possible looking and making offers, you need to advertise in the most effective way. A good Realtor will help, but make it clear what price YOU want out of it. Newspaper ads are good. Most people look there when trying to find a house. If you advertise through the newspaper, use the following as guidelines:

1. Your ads should state first that which will draw the most attention. The price might do that, but it's

usually the financing information that impresses
people. For example, you could start the ad with the
following:

a.   Owner Contract . . .
b.   Small Down . . .
c. $2,000 moves you in tomorrow . . .
d.   No Qualifying . . .
e.   Easy Assumption . . .

This will get people's attention because it states the
terms they are looking for. The balance of the ad
should be just as exciting.

2.   The ads should pre-qualify the house for prospective
buyers.   I've spent too much time on the phone
answering questions when the information could have
been put in the ad. The most common questions to
answer are:

a.   How many bedrooms?
b.   What is the interest rate?
c.   What are the monthly payments?
d.   Is the yard fenced?
e.   How many bathrooms?
f.   What kind of heating?
g.   Is the house near schools?
h.   Is it on one level?
i.   How large is the garage?

Add a variety of other questions from lot size to bus
lines, from how new the roof is to how old the house
is. Be sure to include the address in the ad. When
they call it helps if they've seen the outside before you
meet them there. This prevents you from having to sit
and wait at the house while they drive up for the first
time, and don't stop because they don't like the
neighborhood or the outside of the house.

Take your choice. You can either answer the questions on the phone or put them in the ad. I would
suggest paying an extra $5.00 or so and put in all the
information that will be deciding factors.

3. If you feel that the house will sell best from the outside, then list the address and the times it will be open. I have, on occasion, hired people to be there, so when someone comes, they can be shown around and given a preprinted sheet with all the pertinent information, especially my phone number. Then, if they are interested, an appointment can be made for me to meet them personally.

CERTAINTIES VS. UNCERTAINTIES

From the time you buy a house and move on to fixing it up, you should remember to eliminate uncertainties. People like to hang on to their CERTAINTIES. If they have $5,000 in the bank for a down payment on a house and the house you have to sell is surrounded with questions, they most likely won't buy it.

Let's suppose the bathroom needs some work. That's simple enough, but maybe all kinds of things are going through their minds. How long will it take? How much will it cost? Who can we get to fix it up? The answers to those questions exist, but sometimes that doesn't matter. With too many questions it's easier for them to walk away. Be ready with answers, but first eliminate those things that make people uneasy.

One time I had an excellent young couple that I knew were stable. They had the down payment but were leery of the basement stairs. I agreed to have the stairs repaired the next day. I was selling the house as is, so they agreed to add that cost to the price, but I was the one who took care of the problem. Everyone was happy.

Financing poses another kind of uncertainty. Obviously, most sellers want to get as much down or as high a monthly payment as possible. These terms leave a lot of questions in the buyer's mind, especially with the economic climate the way it is. They don't even know if they'll have a job next year.

What happens if the wife gets pregnant and has to quit work, etc? In order to alleviate many of these questions, you should be aware of them and take as much uncertainty out of the sale as possible.

When explaining the financing terms, write it out on a piece of paper so the figures are recognizable and definite. I've carried on many negotiations on scratch paper which helped avoid questions like, "Did he say what I think he said?" Figures on paper spark negotiations and eliminate error.

If you put a house in the paper for sale and don't specifically list the terms, people are not sure whether you're charging 10 percent, 11 percent, or 15 percent for your interest rate. Also, they're not sure what the monthly payments are going to cost or how much the real estate taxes are. When they show up to start bargaining, they don't know where to start, there are too many uncertainties in their life. If they have $2,000 in their checking account to put down on the house, they are literally afraid to trade the $2,000 for the house that represents too many uncertainties for them, even though it may be a good deal.

Once I had a house for sale that I wanted to move right away because I needed $3,000 for a commitment I made on buying another house. I felt that the house was worth about $36-37,000, but because I wanted to move it quickly, I was willing to sell it for $30,000 with $3,000 down. A lady came to look and really seemed to like it. The second time she came to look at it, she brought a friend and they were spending all their time figuring out where to hang pictures and where to put the furniture. I was there drawing up the papers, figuring out the deal. The payments were going to be $270 a month. At that time she was paying $300 a month for rent and these payments seemed to be right for her.

She was really excited until she talked with her attorney, who asked questions like, "What about the plumbing? Is the furnace modernized?" Before she came back to get answers to these questions, she wanted to back out of the deal. There was nothing I could say to her to get her to change her mind. Even though almost every one of the questions the attorney asked could be answered in the positive, she left. Within a week I was able to sell it for $36,000 with $4,000 down. She had the opportunity for a great buy, but the attorney in this case caused her to lose out.

In summary, the way to eliminate uncertainties is to keep asking yourself questions like, "Would I want this?" "Can I make this easier to understand?" "Are there any uncertainties that can be cleared up?" Houses are purchased to solve people's problems. Have as many solutions on hand as possible.

PEOPLE BUY FOR THEIR REASONS

Long before I started investing, I learned this lesson. But real estate has thrown me some interesting curves. In my early days of selling insurance I'd ask the question, "Tell me, Bill, of all that we have talked about tonight, what point caused you to buy this policy?"

"I never had the chance to go to college," he would say, "and I'm going to make sure that my kids can go whether I'm here or not." I was shocked. I had given him many better reasons for buying—my company was the best, our dividends were highest and our costs were the lowest. I had just mentioned the college aspect in passing and here he was buying it for that reason.

Learn to think like your prospective buyers and do what you think they will like. People buy and sell houses for their own reasons. It's good to second guess, or find out those reasons and use it to your advantage, but sometimes their reasons will surprise you.

For example, one house I bought was a disaster. This is the house, by the way, that made me finally resolve to never deviate from my plan. It needed everything. After putting in $10,000 of my own money, I borrowed $6,000 more from the bank. After four months of working—fixing up the bathroom, painting the house inside and out, putting on a new roof, putting a cement floor in the garage, laying new carpet throughout, re-doing the kitchen cabinets and every other possible thing that can be done to a house (I really made that old place look like it never did before)--it was ready to sell. After it sold, I asked the lady what made her decide to buy. I was waiting for a compliment on all the quality work that was done, so I was set back when she said, "I've always wanted a house with a double stainless steel kitchen sink." I knew she wouldn't have bought it had all the other work not been done but, heck, the kitchen sink was the one thing that was there when I bought it.

It's good to understand this principle, and it's a comfort to know that, generally speaking, a good portion of the average buyers want a lot of the same things. Keep abreast of the popular trends and make your houses appeal to a wide variety of people.

BENEFITS VS. FEATURES

People buy benefits. When selling your houses, stress the benefits. For our purpose here a benefit is something that will only be derived if a person buys and uses the product. A feature stays with the product whether it's purchased or not.

For example, you walk into a car lot and a salesman says, "You ought to buy this car—it has the best engine on the market." Compare that to another salesman saying, "You ought to buy this car. You will save $415 a year in gas because it has the best engine on the market." The best engine on the market will stay with the car but the benefit of saving gas will only come if you buy and drive it.

Let's get back to real estate. "Close to schools" is a feature but, "you won't have to get up every morning and drive your kids to school—they can just walk around the corner," is a benefit. Certain kinds of heating, new roofs, full basements, big yards, deductible interest payments, fenced yards (and hundreds more) can all be stated as benefits. You'll be surprised how quickly people pick up on these things. They'll only trade their hard-earned cash for benefits.

QUALIFY PROSPECTIVE BUYERS ON THE PHONE

Once I advertised a house, it was exciting to start getting phone calls. I would jump up from dinner, leave company, and drop everything I was doing to go show the house. Then, the prospective buyers wouldn't show up, or they needed a bigger place, or it wasn't close enough to Mama. I soon learned to ask a lot of questions on the phone. I have wasted so much gas, not to mention time, that could have been saved had I qualified the prospective buyers over the phone.

Sometimes you won't get "the whole truth and nothing but the truth," even though people think they are being honest. I can't count the times I've stated what I wanted down and, upon being reassured that the amount was no problem, driven over and shown the house. After they'd fallen in love with the house and it was time to draw up the papers, I'd be told, "The down payment is coming from my mother in New Jersey."

After several bad experiences like that, I learned to ask this leading question: "Now, if you like the house, are you in a position to buy it right away?" Having them answer that question opened up the information channel and saved me a lot of time, and them a lot of embarrassment. (I've rarely seen the relative or friend come through.)

ITS BEST LIGHT

In conclusion, a house should be cleaned up and as close to livable as possible. I wouldn't suggest boiling cinnamon water and baking a loaf of bread in the oven of a vacant house to make it seem "just like home," but having it clean and ready to move into is appealing. Sometimes that's all it needs.

CHAPTER

Tips in General

The following sections contain many things I have learned over the years. These tips are given here in an effort to help you make your investing uncomplicated. It's always advisable to keep your life uncluttered, avoiding entanglements which will slow you down.

THE EIGHT CYLINDER APPROACH

An investor constantly needs to ask himself, "What else could I be doing with my money?" It would be easy for me to say, "Only do things according to this plan, and ignore everything else," but that would be irresponsible on my part.

Even though I do feel there is no better plan (in terms of growth and benefits), I also feel that no one should act on only a few spark plugs. The eight cylinder concept here simply means that all investment plans are considered. I would suggest becoming an expert in one (this one) but at least know of the others, and be prepared to use them all if, at the time, they can benefit you.

Let me give you an example. A friend of mine understood the tax advantages of selling on installment sales. He, too, views all other ways as causing time and money delays. In June he put a house up for sale, asking $50,000—one for which he paid $38,000 with $3,000 down, and then put $2,000 into fixing it up. He was asking for $6,000, but someone came along and offered him $13,000 cash for his equity and wanted to take over his $35,000 contract. This changed the purchase price to $48,000. The buyer had the $13,000 in hand. Most of us would have taken this, but he was afraid of the taxes he would have to pay, so he hesitated. He found himself in a rut and, worst of all, he was not asking the right question—what else could he do with that additional money?

An eight cylinder approach would have him looking at this idea and seeing several alternatives. Let's see what he could have done had he taken the $13,000. He felt that it would have thrown him into a higher tax bracket of around 33 percent (or $2,500, which is 33 percent of the $8,000 profit). This would need to be paid to the IRS, leaving him only $5,500 ($8,000 minus $2,500).

I say get all the cash you can if someone offers it. He was planning to get his $5,000 back anyway so let's see what he did with the other $8,000 (which he could use until tax time). He had six months left this year, plus four months next year before his taxes became due. How much could he make in ten months? He immediately bought two houses and sold them within five weeks. He purchased three more and two months later purchased three more. He sold all of these on contract except one. In February a couple wanted to cash him out of that one. He closed that deal in March—clearing $15,800.

He was going to have high taxes on that amount the next year, but he had cash once again to pay the taxes which were due then. He now had seven additional contracts with equities of $94,000—netting him $850 per month. He had enough cash from the February sale to pay the taxes from the deal last June and the little bit that he would have to pay on each of the installment sales. Plus, he had over $6,000 more to do it again.

One other thing—he also got his original $5,000 back on the previous June sale and that, too, was reinvested.

If someone walks in with cash for a house, take it. My approach doesn't preclude this—it encourages it. What it does suggest, though, is that you look for cash in hand and not money that must come from a bank or a father-in-law in New Mexico.

FORMULAS IN PERSPECTIVE

Many moons ago I read about an old, backwoods Indian guide. The story has it that he was sure-footed, tenacious and always got his people through. The only time he didn't was when they didn't follow him. They could stop and camp here and there and swim in the rivers, but if they got too far behind him, they became lost. Apparently he didn't look around often enough to see where they were.

If you were in the market for a guide, what criteria would you establish for choosing one? Would you want one that knew the way? Would you want one that took care of most of the problems? And would you want one that was acting FOR you? The answers to the foregoing questions are obviously "yes." Because we choose our destination by choosing our path, we must take care to choose wisely.

Some investors live by formulas, some live by intuition alone, while most of us live by a combination of both. But because formulas affect us, we should find the answers to the previous questions, and then move forward asking: (a) How am I going to fit in? (b) How do I start, continue and end? (c) How are adaptations made, if needed?

I bring this up because I have seen people who know the formulas and then go into the real world and blow it. One time, when I had a 5-unit place for sale for $80,000 with $8,000 down, a man looked at me and made an offer of $98,500 with $9,000 down. When I came out of shock, I told him I only wanted $80,000, which was a fair price. "No," he said, "I have this formula and after I plug the rents and expenses in, it comes out to $98,500."

"I know, but it's in a rotten part of town," I answered. He insisted on that amount. Either his guide was a wacko or his brain went swimming too long. You probably think I'm making this up, but it is the truth. I thought it was so far out that I didn't want to do business with him. That was the first reason. The second reason cinched it. His formula said I would wait six weeks, giving him time to close another deal and then come up with the money for my down payment. I sold it to someone else.

This taught me a lesson—WATCH OUT. Caution is the password. Ironically some of the most dubious formulas are expounded in the most convincing way. A good comparison is with the ancient Greeks—the person to win the debate wasn't the one who was RIGHT or WRONG, but the one who put across his argument in the most persuasive manner.

I have had run-ins with many people and their formulas, and after watching them, my suggestion is to keep everything in perspective. Keep learning and adapt information you need to your circumstances and establish check points to measure your progress. In short, make your own formula.

EXCHANGES

There are plenty of books that tell the advantages and mechanics of exchanging properties. I agree that it is an excellent way to defer paying taxes. If you have an excellent agent on your team who can handle all the mechanics, it can be an enjoyable and worthwhile transaction.

I hesitate in suggesting this for a small investor until he has some experience. The reason I say this is because exchanges can get complicated. The more people involved, the more entanglements. At one time five or six people were involved with a three-way exchange. I thought we were a bank with all the problems we were causing.

The deal never was consummated because of one small discrepancy. I wish I could have put together some of these exchanges in my early days, but of the four attempts I made, all of them fell through. There were circumstances out of my control that came up and affected them adversely. If you want this tax advantage, do it right. Let a professional set it up and do the leg work.

HAVING YOUR OWN OFFICE

This question comes up repeatedly. Other people must wrestle with it as I did. For a long time I operated out of my basement, but after a year or so I decided to get an office. In hindsight, I wish I'd followed this plan:

1. Only move when you have to. If you can work at home with no interruptions, fine, but if you end up tending kids and running household errands, it's time to remember that you need to concentrate on investing. If you can have privacy in your home, that is ideal.

2. If a move is needed, make it gradually. Don't get into the biggest, nicest place you can. Move to an office where you share services with others who just want a place to hang their hats. Many buildings have small offices surrounding secretarial/receptionist services.

    The benefits are immense. Somebody is always there to answer your phone; someone will greet people coming to see you, and they will be able to perform typing and copying services. This is an invaluable asset. After having my own secretary for a year, I realized that she spent only one hour a day doing actual typing. I could have saved over $500 a month with other arrangements.

    Also, the place I was going to rent wanted nine cents per page for copies which I thought was too high. I knew the price of paper and copy toner was less than two cents a copy, so I leased a copy machine. Lease payments were $110 a month; paper and toner and maintenance were about $20 a month. I had to service the machine daily, buy the paper, call for repairs, etc., to make my 500 or so copies. I thought I was saving all this money until I multiplied 500 by nine cents and came up with $45, not $130.

Additionally, there usually is a nice conference room for your use when sharing space.

Besides paying an employee, you'd have to pay taxes on those salaries to every government agency available. Payment for these shared services is like rent. Plus, if your own secretary is sick, you'll be left with doing the work yourself or trying to find someone else to do it.

3.   If you need a bigger office, you're on your own. Each person has his reasons, most of which, I would say, are not related to investing. There was nothing I was doing as an investor (even when processing six houses a month) that couldn't have been handled by the office arrangements described above.

In summary, move up slowly. Have your team give you feedback on these moves.

BUSINESS CARDS

Just a hint here might make the difference between turning that one extra deal or not. According to the money machine plan, you're in the buy, fix-up, and sell business. To keep that information in front of people, you should have a nice-looking business card stating so.

First, why a nice-looking card? It's simple; people will hang on to it. If it is embossed or has nice art work, it will hang around the top drawer in their buffet until cousin George comes into town next summer and needs a place to stay. Second, state what you do! This information doesn't have to be long. I saw one card that said "Houses" under the man's name. Another one said, "I buy houses," and another one simply said, "Real Estate Investments."

Many times I would make my offer and, if it was not accepted, just leave. On one house I went back a few weeks later and the man came running out. "I wanted to call you, but I couldn't remember your name," he said. "I finally had to sell the house for $1,000 less than your offer. Man, I wracked my brain for two days trying to reach you."

After that experience I carried it one step further and wrote follow-up letters a few days later restating my offer (being sure to include acceptance date) and again writing my phone number.

Whatever you want your card to say and however you want it to look is important, but it's more important to just have something to leave with people. Remember, "Out of sight, out of mind."

P.S. Just for fun you might want to read about Robert J. Ringer's business card in <u>Winning Through Intimidation</u>.

NOTARY PUBLICS

Being a notary public and having friends that are the same could save you countless hours. It's so convenient to be able to take one of your investor friends with you and not have to wait around for everyone to appear before a notary public. Too many things can happen while waiting.

PARTNERSHIPS

Whole books have been written on this subject. I'll just add a little here. "Avoid costly entanglements" takes on so much importance with partnerships. I'm not saying I'm against them. Some have been the key to success for so many people. But before entering into any arrangement consider the following:

1.   Expectations vary greatly. What you say and what your partner hears can be miles apart. Over time, the difference in expectations increases.
2.   Have well-defined goals.
3.   Remember people's situations change. Whereas they might have excess cash today, tomorrow they may be hurting.
4.   There is no ready market for selling limited partner-ships.

Make sure you have exhausted all other possibilities before seeking out partners.

DEBT RATIO

You must be careful when you are buying and selling to make sure you maintain a proper debt ratio. Debt ratio means the percentage of every dollar of assets that represents liabilities. For instance, I felt that it was in my best interest if I could keep my debt ratio under 65 percent, which means that if I had a $100,000 contract receivable, I would like all of my under-lying encumbrances to total no more than $65,000. Now of course this is impossible to achieve on every transaction, but it can be averaged out over many properties. On higher-priced units, it's very hard to maintain that kind of ratio.

Let's say for instance that you have two pieces of property. You sell them and have a net equity of $20,000. In one, it's a small house, your receivable is $25,000 and your payable is $15,000—you have a $10,000 equity and the debt ratio is 60 percent. But let's say this $10,000 in the other house is a receivable of $80,000 and a payable of $70,000. Your liability to asset ratio is over 87 percent. If this ratio gets way out of line, a slight dip in your market area could adversely affect you. Also, if you must use your financial statement, a bad liabilities to assets ratio will stick out like a sore thumb.

For instance, let's say you have a $400,000 net worth, but it shows up as $900,000 in assets with $500,000 in liabilities. That's not bad, but if that same $400,000 showed up as $500,000 in assets and $100,000 in liabilities, it would look a lot better and I'm sure you would feel even more comfortable. Let's go to the other extreme and say that it shows up as $3,000,000 worth of assets and $2,600,000 worth of liabilities. That ratio is totally out of line and, if you are like me, you wouldn't be sleeping too well at night.

It is easy to keep control in this area. Just weigh each transaction to see how it looks individually and as a part of your total picture.

CARRY LEGAL FORMS AND DEEDS

You never know when a good deal will pop up. I carry all necessary deeds with me—if for no other reason than just to show people what we could be signing at the title company. When I make an offer, I am often asked how the sellers are protected and what will happen if I sell the house to someone who doesn't make payments to them. I pull out the appropriate form and go over those provisions to ease their fears.

CHAPTER **16**

Getting the Equity out of Your House

One of the questions I most frequently receive is, "How do I get the equity out of my house?" Another variation of that question is this, "I'm paying too much in taxes. How do I use my equities to buy tax write-offs?" It's with these questions in mind that this chapter is written.

A MYTH PUT TO REST

Let's put to rest the concept that your only asset for starting an investment plan is the equity in your house. It's there all right, and I'm not going to ignore it, but I will put it in proper light.

Here is your house, the one you're working so hard for. The following sentence makes very little investment sense until you look closer: "I want my own house to be free and clear." Ostensibly it looks like you're not maximizing the potential of mortgaging your house to the hilt for the purpose of leveraging into other properties or investments.

Once you look deeper, you realize how important it is to have this one nest egg, this one piece of earth that is yours. Therefore, if the equity in your home must be used, try to do it for a temporary time only.

If You Must

If you feel that your personal residence is your only source of investment funds, there are a few ways to free up the money. However, please don't read this section and run out and start doing this without reading the balance of this chapter.

Before the alternatives are listed, I must state that I realize the complexity of the economic situation. Many traditional approaches have changed, but let's list several and see if something can happen with one of them or a couple in tandem.

Refinance New Mortgages

Banks will let you refinance your home up to a certain percent of its fair market value. Eighty percent is common these days. If your house is worth $70,000, you may get a loan of up to $56,000 (maybe higher in some areas). If your current loan balance is $40,000, this move will free up $16,000. Not bad for a few hours of paperwork, is it?

Let's look at the negative side and then put it in perspective. This new loan means three things may change:
1.   The amount of interest will go up.
2.   The amount of the monthly payment will increase.
3.   The terminology of the new loan papers will probably change. If it follows the trend, much more will now be in the bank's favor.

Are you willing to pay the price? Do you want to trade what you have for this new set of figures?

The answer to this needs to be put in perspective, and the best way to do that is to ask another question: What else could you do with the money?

WHERE'S YOUR PRIORITY?

This is an important question that needs frequent asking. It helps prioritize many things:

- Can I make more money with what I'll get out?
- Am I willing to pay the price in the meantime?
- Can I pay off this excess loan with my profits?
- What happens if the expected profits aren't there, or are longer in coming than anticipated?
- Do I need the whole amount, or can I get by with less?

If you can safely answer these questions, you may proceed in several ways. All of the ways involve some type of additional mortgaging of your house. You could:

- Refinance with a new loan for the whole amount.
- Place a second or third mortgage on the property (Note: the terms of this type of loan are usually more stringent, but these terms only apply to the actual amount of this loan. The first mortgage remains intact with no change.)
- Create notes and mortgages to yourself as a lien against your property and then use them as down payments on other properties.
- Sell your house, thereby receiving the full equity. Part may be used to move into another house with the balance going to investments.
- Trade your property for other property.

Any lending institution can help you prepare these documents. That's the easy part. The hard part is making the decision to go ahead. And before that decision is made, several other things need to be considered.

It Must Be A Good Investment

The first consideration in purchasing any property should be its investment qualities. I have said this many times. Yes, it's important to look at the tax implications, but your first analysis should be to determine if it's a good investment.

However, the opposite is true when trading or selling your house. The first consideration when selling property is to determine the tax ramifications. It's amazing how quickly selling one property affects your tax status on other properties.

You'll need to set the sale of any one property in context with the others. Write it all out. See how the properties you're holding (and thus creating tax write-offs) will affect the sale. See if your proceeds will be used to leverage you into yet another property that may create tax write-offs this year to offset your gain.

Isn't investing exciting? All of these great things to do to get ahead and keep all of your money working for you.

The Law Of Leverage

Making small amounts of money do large amounts of work is a main ingredient of successful investing. We all talk about this, but unless it becomes an integral part of our investing philosophy, this successful law is wasted.

Once you master it, though, you realize that you don't need as much money as previously thought. You can demand less from your house and yet get this lower amount to do more.

If you look at others and think back on your own investing career, were not the best deals made when you were broke? Poor people make great investors. People with money have a tendency to spend it to solve problems. It's the easy road. And then, once this large amount of money is tied up in the property, the property takes charge. It's sad to see people doing things they don't want to do just to free up their money once again.

One more point: once a large amount of money is tied up, people have a tendency to overreact. They start doing things they normally wouldn't do. This is called being emotionally involved. Usually the higher the emotional level, the lower the intellectual level. If you find yourself in this position, seek competent help so you will at least get feedback and build a foundation of contrasting opinions upon which you can base your decision. It is easy to make the law of leverage work for you—pretend that you are poor!

Try a Little First

It is a revelation to some that they do not have to take out all of their money to accomplish a lot. In reality, it is a relief for them to know that they will not have to commit to a whole new life-style because they have taken out a large loan.

One other important point is that people can take out a little and test the waters with different types of purchases and learn what to do when they get larger amounts. Sometimes the job of tying up a large number of properties seems ominous. But look at the alternatives.

If you want to put down large down payments, you are going to spend a lot of time getting at the money and maximizing it, and investment will be tougher. As the weeks pass, you will probably spend much time worrying about the money and, when you try to sell, more time trying to free it up.

On the other hand, if you use very little cash on the downside, the time needed to find the good deals will be more, but two important good points come to mind:
1.   Time is spent with no commitments. You are free to look, to explore, to negotiate; most importantly, you are free to change your mind.
2.   Because very little of your money is tied up, you are in control when it is time to dispose of the property. You are free to sell it or trade it any way you please.

Many people feel that if small amounts are good, big amounts must be better. Maybe so, maybe not. Along with holding large amounts of money comes a large responsibility. Carefully weigh the amount of time you are willing to spend to manage your money effectively.

Creating Tax Write-Offs

Now that we have covered leverage and other aspects of the decision-making process to free up equity for investment capital, it is time to cover a few basic pointers in maximizing your efforts:

- Learn as much as you can about the tax law (The Tax Acts of 1986, 1991, 1993, and more recent ones). Get a functional knowledge of:
  a) The new write-off schedules
  b) The different types of property that may be a part of any real estate purchase
  c) Section 179 property
- Study up on carrybacks and carryovers so you can see how one year's actions affect other years. Be acutely aware of the dates which represent the one year mark for long-term capital gain purposes and any other tax considerations.
- Consider selling your property on installments to avoid large tax liabilities.
- Make sure that you have an up-to-date financial statement.
- Work up a system for having some sort of P & L (Profit and Loss) Statement so you can quickly pinpoint things to do and alternatives for solving problems.
- Become familiar with the terminology of your transactions to know what you are committing yourself to.
- Develop and maintain a good record-keeping system. Put special emphasis on doing what it takes to do your taxes effectively.

- Develop terminology that will let you take the maximum tax write-offs on each purchased property.

A Little More Detail

Let's take a little extra time to cover this last point in more detail. When you buy an average rental property, part of the purchase may include items that can be written off faster.

For example, a $100,000 four-plex may be valued at $80,000 for the building and $20,000 for the land. According to the old system, this would produce approximately $5,000 in depreciation expense which will offset exactly that much in profits and gains from other sources.

By breaking the purchase price down even further, we can value the stove, refrigerator, dishwasher and separate air conditioning unit (all 5-year types of property) at $2,000. Then we can put a valuation on the carpet, drapes, and furniture at $8,000 (3-year types of property). Coupling these new figures with the new write-off schedules will make the average deduction jump from $5,000 to about $9,000. What a great advantage this is. It could be thousands of dollars in actual savings; added to similar write-offs on other properties, the savings could make for a very nice tax liability situation.

The following phrase can be used in every purchase you make. Even if you plan to sell the property, things happen to alter the plans, so make it a part of every offer:

"The valuation of different types of property of this purchase price will be established between the buyer and the seller before closing."

You may then write down the values of each of these types of property and make the list a part of the closing documents. Make sure both the buyer and the seller sign it. If values are established by an independent appraiser, the clause above could read:

"The valuation of different types of property of this purchase price will be established by an independent

appraisal. The cost of this appraisal will be paid by
_____."

Now that this is done, the tax calculations are relatively
simple. The IRS form has you list the values placed on these
different units. The savings are tremendous for such little
effort.

PROBLEM-SOLVING

The following section explains a step-by-step procedure
which may be used to solve all sizes of problems. Let's use a
small problem to see how it works: We have a duplex with a
$100 monthly negative cash flow. We want to make it break
even. We don't want to sell it.

STEP 1: Look at the property itself. Is there anything
we can do to raise the income or lower the expenses?

STEP 2: Look to other property that we own. Is there
anything we can do to raise the income and/or lower
the expenses on any of our other properties. Note:
Lowering expenses for Step 1 and Step 2 could involve
renegotiating the debt service (monthly payments) on
existing loans.

STEP 3: Look to new property. Could we purchase other
property with a positive cash flow (other rentals or
even discounted mortgages)? Could we buy and sell
on contract a piece of property which would then
provide positive cash flow with limited tax liabilities?

STEP 4: Look at your tax situation. Is there anything we
can do to maximize our tax write-offs on this and other
properties, to free up money that would be going to the
I.R.S.? This step involves using steps 1, 2 and 3 along
with looking at two other ideas: (a) Checking your W-
2 status. Are you claiming all the dependents you are
entitled to claim? (b) Keeping better records. How
many small items do you buy to handle your rental

units, how many tanks of gas are used up, and how many other expenses are paid without being properly posted so as to be written off?

STEP 5: Look to yourself. Is there anything else that we can do to earn more or spend less?

STEP 6: Look to others. If all else fails and the situation justifies it, look to banks or partners for help.

These steps should be worked in this order. Yes, they can often be used in conjunction with each other. The basis for establishing priorities is found in these steps. If followed, they will open up doors as your mind expands and you get good at conceptualizing blockbusting solutions.

Rome Was Not Built in a Day

Don't fall under the misconception that you will make a million by the end of the week. Build your fortune one brick at a time. Surround yourself with others who can help. Move cautiously, and then only after exploring several alternatives.

Remember, your investments will have to stand the test of time. Almost all of what you do will pass to your family estate with few hitches if it is handled properly. If you think about this for a minute, two other points become clear:

1. The fact that you have done things properly to outlast you means that if you are ever disabled or laid up, your affairs will be easy to manage.

2. Even if nothing drastic happens to you, doing things right will free up your time from putting out fires so you can spend it the way you want.

You will not have to confront uncomfortable memories down the road. Stop, take a look around, and invest your time and energy in doing the right things.

Because investing in real estate is so profitable, the tax implications need to be taken into account at every step. Do

investing in Real Estate is profitable

not wait until April 14 to figure out what and how you have done. Plan your work, then work your plan.

Skinning the Cat

If this chapter does nothing but stimulate your thinking, it will be a success. The fine points are nice to know, but sometimes realizing things in a general way will help just as much, because our only limitation is our lack of imagination.

Knowing this, we are free to explore alternatives. Knowing this also gives us the confidence to seek out professionals and then ask them pertinent questions. It is good to learn from our mistakes, but much wiser to learn from the mistakes of others. In short, there are many ways to skin a cat and there are many ways to achieve your investment goals.

RAMIFICATIONS

It is sad to see people worrying and fretting so much over problems that could have been avoided or solved by a little forethought. Nobody wants to spend his whole time stamping out fires, but far too often this is what many investors spend their time doing. Make sure you take time to do things right. Surround yourself with competent people to help you through problem areas.

It is important for all of us to realize that we are the only ones who control our future. Do not expect everything to go right. Murphy is everywhere and the only way to beat him is to be a step ahead of him. A step ahead where we can plan for the unexpected and take the necessary precautions to keep everything going in the right direction.

Publisher's Note

We would like to make a special offer to those of you who have purchased this book.

Many of you will not be able to attend the dynamic seminar that Mr. Cook teaches around the country. But we would like to give you a sampling of what it is like to be there, with a free hour-long tape covering all these concepts of buying, holding, and selling properties. It includes "The Three Entity Approach," the retirement portion of Mr. Cook's whole system of investing in real estate, and is called, "Everything You Ever Wanted To Know About The Real Estate Cash Flow Boot Camp."

Alternately, you may want to order either the "Tri-pak" starter tape set, or the full "Wealth Institute", a 10-volume cassette series on real estate investing. For prices on either, call the order number 1-800-872-7411.

For your free tape or any other inquiry, write:

United Support Association, Inc.
24837 104th Ave. SE
Suite 201
Kent, WA 98031

CHAPTER **17**

My Real Estate Agent Loves Me

When I became serious about real estate investing, I felt I needed to surround myself with a dedicated, up-beat team of professionals. I needed people who not only could put together creative deals for me, but who would be flexible when it came to their own interests.

When my program heated up, I was purchasing two to five houses a month. It was hard to continually find houses to fix up and quickly resell. To keep up this volume, the idea to "buy right (low) in order to sell right" became all-important. Often the only thing that stood in the way was the large down payment required to close in order to cover commissions.

THEN I MET MORT

At this time I met an agent named Mort. He was aggressive and had good business sense. We closed a traditional deal wherein he received the customary six percent commission. We got to know each other pretty well during the paperwork and I found out he was ready to go on his own, as he had just passed his broker exam. At this time, though, he had an arrangement to pay $300 a month for office expenses and use of another broker's services, but not having to split commissions.

Mort and I went to lunch one day and hashed out an investment strategy. The idea was that Mort would find properties for me and then take his commissions on contract. (Actually we used a deed of trust.) The terms of the contract would be that the monthly payments would be one percent repay, meaning that if the commissions were $2,000, the monthly payment would be $20. All notes were to bear an interest rate of 11 percent.

Both of us were reluctant at first. I didn't want to impose on him because I knew how important getting cash would be to running his business. He had the same fears, but took the attitude that he would squeeze in a few deals for me in between his regular activities.

Things Picked Up

After about a week, he called with several houses to go look at. I made offers on four and two were accepted. His commissions were $2,800 and $4,900, and the next month he started receiving his $28 and $49 checks.

During this time he had one other house close and that kept him going. In the second month he found two more houses and a third by the end of the month. The first two closed and his net income picked up by another $95. He needed some cash so he discounted the very first $2,800 note for 60 percent of its face value, netting $1,680. At the end of his second month he had:

- Cash of about $1,800 (from sale of the contract plus the other monthly payments)
- Equities of $14,400
- Monthly payments still coming in at $144 per month
- A sale on one other house that he had found for me but that I didn't buy
- A sale on one other house to me that would be closing the next month

Now We're Cooking

Already Mort was taking a second look at this M.O. (modus operandus). He put me on the front burner and both of us started cooking. He took me to lunch again for the prime purpose of asking me if I could pick up my purchases to four a month instead of two.

I told him that I would have to close the deals more quickly and always get the keys upon acceptance of earnest money (if the properties were vacant). He found a different escrow and title officer who could process the transactions in two or three days. We were in business.

Two days later we looked at eleven properties. I made offers on eight. Mort said that four of the eight were really shaky, but because he was taking his commissions on notes, it left almost all of the down payments free to go to the sellers. He literally plastered together four of the deals. These eight were all small houses, but still his commissions totaled $25,600, netting another $256 a month.

Activity Breeds Activity

There must be something to the expression that activity breeds activity. It seems that the sheer volume of these transactions created other sales for Mort. He was beating the streets for me and uncovered two other houses that sold to others and closed within two months. This happened month after month. Mort sowed and then reaped more than he had ever imagined possible.

By this time a lot of things started happening; so many, in fact, that I couldn't keep track of them. I knew about deals that he was putting together for me, but had no idea of all the other properties that he was processing because of these contracts.

I don't know all that he did, but we talked often enough for me to find out the following:

One day he came across four 4-plexes that required $5,000 down. The man wanted Mort to sell them for him. Mort knew a good deal when he saw one and attempted to buy them for himself. The man was a doctor and was to the point of exasperation with the tenants and his managers, and seriously wanted to unload them. He would have taken zero down, but he wanted to make sure that his buyer had something to lose if he or she walked away.

Hence the $5,000. The purchase price was $300,000, which was even below market value. Mort didn't have the $5,000 cash but he sure didn't want this one to get away. He knew too many things could happen with even a two or three day delay. He made an offer to the doctor of $10,000 down, using three contracts (actually totaling $10,450 when the exact figures were researched).

Mort Used His Head

He told the doctor of his 60 cents on the dollar sale, and also mentioned that the profit portion of the monthly payments from these contracts would be able to be claimed as received. They both agreed and the papers were drawn.

The doctor carried the contract on the balance and Mort now had 16 units which were all full, except one. The doctor had trouble worrying about the places, but not Mort. He moved his wife and himself into the vacant unit, and almost immediately started making over $800 a month off the rents besides the tremendous tax benefits.

His Dream House

The second big thing that happened to Mort happened right after he moved into the 4-plex—he found his dream house. Both Mort and his wife were exhausted from moving, but they would have done anything to get into this house.

Unfortunately, the seller was about as creative as a big bank; the only thing he wanted was cash for his equity and the underlying loan was not assumable in any way, shape or form. It had as many clauses as Macy's at Christmas time.

The only solution was a new mortgage. Things didn't look so good. Mort had everything going against him during the first half of the loan interview. Since he'd been a broker for only a short time, his income wasn't that steady, and most of all, this savings and loan didn't like real estate agents. He thought he was wasting his time, but then the loan officer started asking about his other assets.

A Change in Atmosphere

He brought out his portfolio of contracts and rentals and paraded them in front of her and the whole atmosphere changed. Remember, Mort had only been operating like this for about five months but already his contract and rental equities totaled over $160,000. The loan officer almost got dizzy turning around so fast! The loan was approved. They moved in a week later.

I didn't mention the other exciting aspect of this deal. The house was worth $125,000. The seller was afraid of the market and also needed to move, since his company had already transferred him. He offered to lower the price to $90,000 for Mort if he could get the deal within a month. It took only three weeks and everyone walked away with a smile.

Trading Contracts

Mort had sold four other houses to me by this time. He took these contracts and traded them on a 12-plex. I don't know all the details. I asked him about it once and he just smiled. Mort had a knack for finding a good deal, usually in real estate, but sometimes in cars. He found a man with a Mercedes for sale at a price way under value. The owner wanted $4,000 cash, but took one of Mort's $5,000 contracts instead. Thus he could claim the profit on an installment sale. Mort drove away in a nice Mercedes.

"Creamy" Deals

I know that several times other agents would throw good deals at him because they weren't flexible enough with the agent/broker relations to swing them and in would walk Mort to get the cream. As a matter of fact, his activities led him into so many creamy deals he could have opened a dairy. Once in a while he would invite other agents to sell properties. If they needed cash for their commissions, he would make arrangements to pay them and take the whole contract himself.

Unfortunately, all investors run into problems. Mort was sued by a tenant. The matter was solved before any litigation in the courtroom, but $920 was chalked up in lawyer fees. Mort didn't want to pay him in cash so he gave him a $1,400 contract. Everyone was happy.

Mort was now to the point that he started buying contracts. He would find houses for me and try to get those having underlying loans to discount the equity and sell them to him.

One other thing that needs to be mentioned here is that Mort was able to claim his commissions as income as he received them (treated like installment sales). He also received the benefits from some of the contracts as if they were cash in some of his trades. It was great to see that even after all his wheeling and dealing, he still paid taxes.

Pioneering the System

Many other agents wanted to get involved with him and with me. They could see the large volume of activity that we were creating. Mort wanted all of this business himself. He felt he had pioneered a new system that others had laughed at. Now he was making good money and he wanted to keep it that way. While his cohorts were running around doing the bidding of banks and government agencies to get one deal closed, he was closing five to six. He felt it was his gold mine and guarded it carefully.

Economic necessity or financing restrictions have posed a real problem for some agents and forced them to move in this direction. The ones that see the whole picture and utilize this method along with their other activities stack the deck in their favor. Mort didn't want me to let the cat out of the bag, but it needs to be let out. Creativity indeed has become the byword.

Parting of the Ways

I don't see much of Mort these days. We've both moved on to bigger and better things. The last time that I heard from him, he was doing a lot of traveling, looking at big complexes all over the country.

We both learned a lot from each other. We used to joke about the expression, "If you'll do for two years what most people won't do, you'll be able to do for the rest of your life what most people can't do." He made it come true. He was a dealer who wanted to hold all the cards, and he did. Together we stumbled on a way that let him build up his deck faster than either of us thought possible.

My Real Estate Agent

Years later people still ask about Mort's success. His own words sum it up best: "Now I have a steady income, security, travel and a great financial statement. Had I remained a 'traditional' Realtor, I'd still be working 60 hours a week to get a few sales closed. Now I have all the freedom I want."

"Agents, even if it's coming in bite-sized pieces, it's better than what you had coming in yesterday."

BOB STEELE, REAL ESTATE BROKER AND LECTURER

CHAPTER **18**

The Three Entities

Necessity is the mother of invention. So much of what I accomplished in my early years of investing was done by the hit-and-miss, try, back up and try again method. Sometimes I wondered if I would ever get ahead. Luckily, the information I needed to continue the process of achieving my goals was also supplied.

As I started having some success in one area, it seems that problems would crop up in other areas. Many a good book has been written to get people started investing and give the "how to's" of putting certain deals together. So most often, when I needed information, I could go to a book or to a professional and get the specific help I needed.

But it became apparent that even after achieving only modest success, I would need a comprehensive system of investing in real estate, a system to address these problems:

- Generating and maintaining positive cash flows.
- Sheltering income through long-term installment sales and depreciation expense.
- Providing security for the future. (Who wants to rely on social security?)
- Keeping current income (cash) working for the previous three without being swallowed in the IRS abyss.

- Finding a way of working hard for a while, then slowing down and directing my assets to beat inflation.

Sound like a tall order? It was just that. But I also realized that maintaining assets is almost as hard as building them up. So I had no alternative but to find a plan that worked.

There is no college class for the real estate investor to take. Yes, there are books and seminars available, and I encourage reading and taking as many of these as possible. However, what is really needed is more comprehensive than any one or two of these. Don't get me wrong. I'm not putting down attempts to buy with no money down, or the idea of papering your way to millions, or equity participation or any of the other hosts of strategies that rise and fall in popularity. All of these are good as stepping stones. They should be viewed as tools. It is important to have the most modern, up-to-date tool chest possible. But once successful, I wasn't in need of specific techniques, but a whole system. What will be explained now is an A to Z system for investing in real estate that encompasses these good, honest methods and puts them to work for your total financial security.

THE START OF THE SYSTEM

I was becoming quite successful with my properties and started worrying about my long and short-term tax liabilities. It was to answer this tax question that I started the search to find a "total concept" for my investment.

One lesson I had to learn too many times was to concentrate my energies on one thing. Many of the popular non-real-estate, tax-shelter ideas weren't good for me. My expertise was growing with small properties and I wanted to capitalize on my knowledge and experience. There was no time to start over in a different field.

I spent a whole afternoon listening to an insurance agent/investment counselor expound the virtues of tax-shelter investment opportunities. I tried hard to find the good in them. But when I matched his *annual* investment returns with my *weekly* and *monthly* returns, they couldn't compare. I would do better to keep my money working and pay the taxes.

He then listened to me for a while. He could see where I had come from and the growth I was having, and he candidly told me I needed a corporate pension and profit sharing plan (hereinafter called the PLAN). Hungry for new information, I pressed him for more. What he told me was almost too good to be true.

Before we get into the specifics of the PLAN, let me first mention that you need not incorporate to establish a PLAN. You should, however, seriously look at NEVADA as your state of incorporation. It is by far the best. If you want more information send $14.95 to U.S.A., 24837 104th Ave. SE, Suite 201, Kent, WA 98031. We will send a complete Seminar and Instruction Kit. Call 1 800 872 7411 for faster service.

Some Specifics

I have devised a system for finding good deals, then selling them on a wraparound basis in an attempt to:

- Recover my down payment and fix-up costs so I could do it again.
- Build up a strong, steady net income from turning many properties this way.
- Spread out my tax liabilities over the 25 to 30 years of the wraparound mortgage by claiming my gain on the installment sales method.

This plan worked well and became the income-generation part of the whole system. Also, creating it let me move on to a more sure way of protecting my assets and helped me learn how to invest in several types of properties and transactions.

THE PLAN

I left this agent's office as excited about what he told me as anything I've ever been excited about. I immediately made an appointment with my attorney to check it all out. Let me give you the gist of what the PLAN can do so you can see how it fits into the picture.

Once incorporated, you use your corporation to buy and sell properties. It needs to start fresh and go out and make a profit. This can be done by any of the techniques you've learned. It can buy with zero down; it can lease option properties; it can form equity participation agreements; it can assume FHA and VA loans. In short, it can do what you can do. It is a legal entity with a life of its own.

It's easy to get it started. Once done, you just buy properties in the corporation's name. If you are new at this, it would be advisable to seek competent professional advice. Do it right so you can avoid headaches later on.

Now that the corporation is operating on its own and making a profit, it can take a percentage (up to 25%) of the money available for wages and put it into the PLAN. What is this "money available for wages?" It's not the net profit that is calculated after taking out the wages. It is all the money available for wages after subtracting the normal expenses. For example, let's say your corporation made $80,000 gross by turning six properties this year. Let's say the costs of doing business total $20,000. You now subtract the $20,000 from the $80,000 and that leaves $60,000 available for salaries. Maybe your salary to yourself and a few employees totals $45,000. You would think the percentage would then be on the $45,000 paid out; but it's more than that. The percentage is calculated on the whole $60,000, which comes to $15,000. That's $15,000 that can be put into the PLAN.

This donation to the PLAN becomes an immediate tax write-off to the corporation. So now the corporation pays fewer taxes. As a matter of fact, continuing with the same example, our $80,000 gross income is lessened by the $20,000 expenses, the $45,000 in salaries and the $15,000 in donations to the PLAN. That leaves zero income to the corporation which means no tax liability.

More on the PLAN

What is the Pension and Profit-Sharing Plan? It's a separate legal entity set up and recognized by the IRS for the benefit of the retirement of the employees of your corporation. It is a trust that is a living, thriving entity. It can do many things, and the beauty of it is that you can be the trustee and control where the money is invested.

Where does the money go? It goes into the PLAN's checking or savings account. It is then available for investing. You, as the trustee, decide what types of properties it will buy (or sell). In short, it can do just about what you can do with one major exception: all of the money in the PLAN can be turned over time and time again. The PLAN can buy and sell investments and make thousands and thousands of dollars— it can even grow into millions—TAX FREE. The PLAN will never pay taxes.

What happens to this money? It just stays in the PLAN investing or earning interest until you decide to retire. Let's say you turn 54 or whatever age, declare your retirement, and you begin to take out $3,000 a month to live on. You will now have to claim that income as it is taken out and claim it in your then current tax bracket. (You'll then need to buy a few rental properties to create enough depreciation expense to offset this amount.)

I've just given the highlights here. Sound good? It's the greatest tax shelter I've ever seen and the PLAN I've just described (Money Purchase Plan) is the most modest of the ones available. (They include Defined Benefit and Defined Contribution Plans—ask a Pension and Profit-Sharing Plan Administrator for details.)

THREE ENTITIES

Over the years I've developed the three-entity approach to investing in real estate. The three entities are the corporation, the individual, and the pension and profit-sharing plan. Don't let this sound complicated. I firmly believe in keeping things simple. This whole system has simplicity at its core and has a goal of progressing rapidly in the present while setting up a foundation for long term wealth accumulation and retention.

The Corporation's main objective is twofold. It is the entity that makes profits to pay me a salary and it puts money into the PLAN as a tax write-off. It's income comes from capital gains and interest income generated on the loans (mortgages, deeds of trust, etc.) that you create or buy and then carry. By effectively paying out all of its income, the corporation has no tax liability.

The individual has a main objective of eating and sleeping comfortably. With the excess salary received from the corporation, we invest in income-producing properties which create the depreciation expenses and the NOL (net operating loss) to offset this same income (and possibly income in other tax years), thereby allowing us to avoid paying taxes.

The PLAN's goal is to grow at a faster rate than the other two can grow and provide income and security for our future. The PLAN is so exciting, and because this chapter is about how the three work together and not all of the details on any specific entity, I refer you to another publication. I have written extensively on the PLAN in a publication called the Three Entity Approach to Investing in Real Estate—which also has a prototype plan that has already been approved by the IRS. (See ordering information in the back of this book.)

Working Together

Once the three entities are in place (and it could take two to three months to set them up), you are ready to grow faster than you've ever thought possible. If handled right, none of the entities will have to pay taxes—leaving all of your cash available for more investing. Isn't that exciting? You'll once again feel like you're back in control.

Let's see how they work together on a specific deal. When the earnest money agreement (offer to purchase) is signed, you, as the purchaser, should be, "John D. and Mary J. Doe, husband and wife, or their assigns." Your offers should have this so you can assign the transactions to either the corporation or the PLAN on or before closing the transaction. You'll not always know which one of your entities should be buying the property and this will give you time to decide.

Which one will buy it? That depends on several things. I firmly believe in not leaving money tied up in a property. I don't want my cash to become equity. If the deal requires a down payment and fix-up costs, then I want either the corporation or the PLAN to buy it. I turn and sell this type of property and I want the profits (probably short-term capital gain) to be in one of these two entities.

Which one of the two should receive the profits? That depends on which one has money at the time, or which one I'm actively working with at the moment. Obviously, I would like to be spending all of my time developing the tax-free asset growth of the PLAN, but I need to live, so the corporation needs to continue to create an income. The need to be actively working the corporate assets will go down as it creates more steady income. But in the beginning, you'll have to look closely at which entity will do the buying.

If the purchase requires little or no money down and very few repairs and has a positive or break-even cash flow, then the property is a prime candidate to be held for the long term. I buy this property as an individual. This lets me take advantage of the depreciation expense when I sell it, and take advantage of long-term capital gains.

Buying long-term rental properties and selling only once in a while keeps my status as an investor and not a dealer. The properties that will be turned right away can go under the corporation or the PLAN. A corporation is a dealer anyway, but installment sales treatment will prolong the tax ramifications on almost all of my deals. Please refer to Chapter 9 for details.

As I mentioned before, this is a whole system of growth. The beauty is no tax, yet rapid growth. And the whole system can be done with any business that you're in. Real estate works so well and is a natural for the three entities because of the income generation attribute, the growth potential, and the tax shelter aspect already there to enhance each of the entities.

And because it is a complete system, any of the entities can use any of the techniques for buying, fixing up, holding, and selling of real estate--the tools you need to start and maintain your own investment system.

Let's put this down graphically so you can see how the entities affect each other.

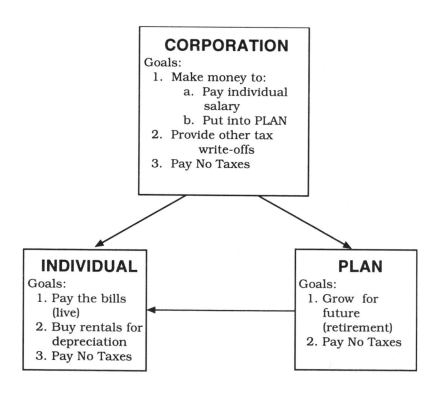

CORPORATION
Goals:
1. Make money to:
   a. Pay individual salary
   b. Put into PLAN
2. Provide other tax write-offs
3. Pay No Taxes

INDIVIDUAL
Goals:
1. Pay the bills (live)
2. Buy rentals for depreciation
3. Pay No Taxes

PLAN
Goals:
1. Grow for future (retirement)
2. Pay No Taxes

CHAPTER **19**

Be a Monomaniac

No better advice can be given than to specialize. Great men who left their mark in life targeted their efforts—they were monomaniacs. Thomas Edison once said, "You and I each have eighteen hours we can spend doing a number of different unrelated things. I spend it doing just one thing, and some of my work is bound to amount to something."

One of the most famous men to study management said:

> The single-minded ones, the monomaniacs, are the only true achievers. The rest, the ones like me, may have more fun; but they fritter themselves away . . . Whenever anything is being accomplished, it is being done, I have learned, by a monomaniac with a mission . . . The rest of us, with multiple interests instead of a single mission, are certain to fail and to have no impact at all.
> —*Adventures of a Bystander*
> Peter F. Drucker, Harper Colophon Books

That's pretty hard on most of us, so let me tone it down with a qualification. I agree with Mr. Drucker, and I categorize myself with him; that is, I am not a monomaniac. Being a monomaniac doesn't mean that a person can't have any other interests, but it does mean that he shouldn't do more than one thing at a time. This is an important difference. It boils down to this—success comes from concentrating one's energies. That energy can be targeted in only one direction at a time. If you want to move on to something else, burn the bridge and move on wholeheartedly.

I had another friend who had a similar experience but he could never make the break. Over the two years that I watched him, he made three times as much investing as he did in his business, but he couldn't zero in on either one. Consequently he floundered from one crisis to another—and neither one did very well.

AN EXPERT ON ONE THING AT A TIME

The question, "Can a man serve two masters?" has timely importance here. There's a real tendency to think that if you're a real estate investor, you're an investor in every sense of the word. Take a few embarrassing pages out of my history. At times I felt in control of the whole money market and wanted to become a financial expert. I invested money in mutual funds and even purchased some bonds. It would have taken five years to get the kind of return on them that I could have obtained in real estate in a few weeks, but I was going to be a financial expert. Now I realize that people spend years becoming experts in those areas. In my naivete, I assumed that because I was successful in one area, I had a free ticket in all other areas. How wrong I was!

Becoming an expert in any field requires either a little effort over an extended time or an all-out effort over a short time. But what is important is becoming the expert. To do this, you need to stick to one thing.

DIVERSIFY OR DIE

The pyramid-shaped building you see in San Francisco stands for diversification, and it's apparent how successful that company is. But we don't see all the companies that have failed because of too much diversification. There was a time when it was considered prudent to diversify—for tax purposes, growth, protection, etc. Now, a lot of those same companies are cutting back—ridding themselves of these other interests. Diversification causes new management problems and puts an excessive drain on the main company.

For us, individually, there is a time when we ask the same question, "Should we diversify?" I answered "yes" to that question, and it started me on a downhill slump.

I was heavy into investing and because I wanted to be at the office more, I started a rental location service. It was draining my cash, but since the secretary was there, I also started another business. This one was a telephone answering service. I also reactivated my insurance agency to write insurance on all of my properties. These businesses started consuming my time. For six months I didn't buy one house. Then I took another step in the wrong direction. I started a major advertising business and sold several of my real estate contracts to support it. I wasn't able to give my all to any of these businesses that were crying for my attention. Finally, I realized the money for me was strictly in real estate. I had spent a long time developing these talents. With this realization I dissolved everything but the real estate. Hindsight is easy and, if I could, I would change most of what I did during that time. Why quit doing that which is successful?

Don't Quit Doing That Which Is Successful

We all have tendencies to do this. I had a friend who sold thingamajigs. His sales would be modest until he attended a sales convention somewhere like Bermuda. He'd come back all fired up and become the top salesman. After five or six months the high volume would stop and he'd be back to his old ways. Then he'd go to another convention in Hawaii and the process would repeat. We talked about this one day and I asked him why this happened. He said he hadn't really noticed, but now that I mentioned it, he wondered too. Many people have answers for his behavior, but I said it seemed to me that his motivation came from the outside and not the inside. It's a lesson for all of us. When we're on track, we should be like a horse with blinders on and not quit or get sidetracked while we're still in the race.

Ask the Right Questions

One of the most important things in becoming an expert investor is to ask the right questions. It's easy to put a lot of importance on having the right answers but too often they could be the right answers to the wrong questions. Both of my friends mentioned before were intelligent and had a strong desire to get ahead. I heard the questions they asked themselves. The first friend, the one who couldn't make the break, kept asking, "Does the money from investing help my business, and does the steadiness of my business help my investing?" The Realtor friend asked, "In what area will I get the greatest return for my time and cash investment?" You can see by their answers which had the effective question.

Don't stop because you might not have the right questions. In lieu of having the right questions, ask a LOT of questions. If you do this, eventually you will learn how to ask the right questions. When the right questions are asked, then the right information can be received in its proper light. It's like a giant computer—the answers are there, we just have to learn how to get at the information. Once this process becomes a way of life to the investor, the next step is to keep learning and adding current information to the stockpile. Usually this opens up new questions, and it's this pursuit of excellence that makes for successful investing.

I'm reminded of a story about Albert Einstein sitting next to an eighteen-year-old girl at a banquet. After a while she asked him what he did for a living. When he replied, "I'm engaged in the study of physics," she responded, "Oh, that. I studied that last semester!" Learning is an everyday necessity in everything we do, especially when we desire to be successful at what we are doing.

DECISION-MAKING—POLICY-MAKING

Decision-making and policy-making are the jobs of the executive. He needs to be a thinker. If he has properly surrounded himself with the right people and the right information, then his task will be easier. He must realize that the decision-making process starts with gathering opinions—hopefully conflicting opinions. Most of us gather facts to substantiate our beliefs. If you don't have contrasting opinions, you won't see all the sides. Don't make any decisions until you hear the opposing position. Build your decision on a foundation of contrasting opinions.

It's almost trite to say that there are two kinds of knowledge—that which you have and that which you have access to. No single person can know all there is about investing because there's too much to learn and it's constantly changing. Therefore, it behooves us to surround ourselves with a good team—people that are experts in their field, who know how to ask the right questions and where to look for the right answers.

The last thing an investor needs is "yes" people in his life, because they will cause more harm than good. I found myself with people like this at times. Because there was so much going on—homes, rentals, contracts, repairs—they would be awed by it and nod their heads up and down at almost anything I wanted to do. I knew that I wasn't getting the proper negative feedback to help keep me on track. I wanted a challenge now and then to keep me thinking of alternatives.

Luckily, I had a couple of friends that took everything I

said with a questioning attitude. "Are you sure that's your only alternative?" That doesn't seem like it follows your plan." "You're like a saw that never stops. You'd better get away from it and sharpen your blade." This is the kind of questioning I needed. I took those few friends to lunch often so I would have someone to throw a bucket of cold water on me when I needed it. Choose this team wisely—they could make or break you.

Make sure you have on your team:
1. One good real estate agent/broker
2. A knowledgeable escrow and/or title officer
3. A dependable real estate attorney (one who will be there when you need him)
4. A good tax consultant
5. A good friend or two (another investor, if possible).

Knowledge

There is no substitute for on-the-job training. Before I got into real estate investing, I owned a small ice cream parlor where I learned what I needed to know from DOING.

I didn't have a degree in business, or anything else that would help in this endeavor. Advertising, ordering, customer relations, hiring and firing, and all the other skills I needed to be successful at that time came by asking the right questions to the right people. Also, I tried, made mistakes, and tried again. No formal education could have given me all I learned, and I wouldn't trade those few years of experience for an MBA. The knowledge I gained has carried over into almost all other facets of my life.

I'm reminded of the story of a young reporter talking to a successful corporate executive.

"Why are you so successful?"

"Two words, son, two words—right decisions."

"And how did you learn to make right decisions?"

"One word, son, one word—experience."

"And how did you get experience?"

"Two words, son, two words—wrong decisions."

My hope is that you can see how this applies to real estate investing. If so, I'm confident that you are on the road to success.

Take Time Off

Another important question keeps surfacing: "When should an investor take time off?" That isn't an easy question to answer if your situation becomes like mine did.

The life you lead as an investor is an extremely exciting one. In fact, it is so exciting that you'll have trouble finding recreational activities that compare. Watching TV will be boring, and you'll find yourself starting to fall asleep at the movies (unless it's a good Clint Eastwood movie). So my work became my hobby—I spent many hours thinking only of houses. It was all that I was interested in and it started to consume me. Before long, I was so wrapped up in the day-to-day details that I couldn't see the big picture. I couldn't make sure that I was continuing to operate in an effective manner—making sure that my cash could pay the bills and keep the program going. I started worrying about little things, instead of the whole concept. I had to force myself to take time out and get away from it—really get away.

I asked myself, "Does the corporate executive take time off?" "Yes," I thought. He goes golfing and takes vacations. There was a period of time when I was so busy that I started making too many wrong decisions. Now when I look back, I see how tired I was. I realized I had to get away from it. It's like a child who plays all day, then denies that he's tired. If the much-needed rest doesn't come, you can't think straight. I do not claim to be an expert on the subject, but I know from experience that this kind of work requires constant brain power—and the brain needs to be recharged now and then. There's no good time to leave this business. Just set your dates, take your spouse, and go. It will all be there when you get back. And remember you can take several two or three - day trips instead of a long vacation. If you love this work, you'll love it even more if you can get away from it now and then.

In the movie "The Fiddler on the Roof," the father was constantly faced with questions that, for him, should have been easy to answer because he had tradition to guide him. But the questions needed new answers or at least a re-evaluation of the old premises. At first, when confronted with these problems, he balked. Then the camera would zoom him off to the other side of the bridge or a field and he would carry on a conversation as if talking with God. He would come to a decision and then zoom back and solve the problem.

Wouldn't it be great if we could all do that? We can, to some extent. I used to go for rides, or to the park—even just for a few hours. Be fresh and you won't get slapped.

THE OVERRIDING CONCEPT OF SUCCESS

Now that you are a monomaniac, becoming an expert, asking the right questions, setting up your team, learning every day, and taking the proper time off, we can tie it all into another concept—the overriding concept that determines success or defeat. In order to do this, let's return to Peter Drucker for his comments on being effective. (I'll paraphrase.) He states that the effective executive is one who has the ability to get the right things done, and not necessarily one that always does things right. (*The Effective Executive*, Peter F. Drucker, Harper & Row Publishers.)

When I first understood this concept, I was a little sad. I remembered all the times I had the emphasis turned around. How many costly delays were caused by my putting too much emphasis on doing things right? Now, don't think that I would scrimp on doing something the right way. Our motto in fixing something up was to do it as if we were moving in. But as the executive of my plan, I should have always been doing the right things.

For example, I agree that employee relations are important and I always found time to converse with the people working with me, but one day I went to one of my houses that was having a roof put on and had a revealing experience. There were several guys up on the roof. After exchanging greetings, one of them said, "Hey, grab a hammer and come up and listen to some good jokes." I love good jokes, so it was hard for me to say, "If I do that, I won't be doing my work and you'll be out of a job."

CONCLUSION

Running around at a dizzying pace means nothing unless you're building and achieving. Keep things in perspective and build on the good talents you have as an individual—put your personality into it. The development of good executive attributes will pave the way for your success.

CHAPTER 20

Put the Machine on Automatic Pilot and Retire

Now that you're flying high and want to reap the rewards of your investing, you must capitalize not only on the cash income you have created, but also on the talents and knowledge you have gained.

The plan needs to have a built-in way for you to slow down but keep comfortably ahead. This method has an automatic pilot feature which can be turned on for continued income and growth.

Automatic pilot doesn't mean you can get out of the pilot's chair and sit back in first class for the rest of the trip. It means that you can use your time elsewhere as long as you stay near the controls.

If you think at some given age you will be able to turn your money over to someone else and have them perform with it the way you would, then you don't understand the nature of people. Your highest rates of return on your money will be made when you are there managing it. No matter how you invest your money, you need to keep control. The further you remove yourself from control of your money, the less you should expect to earn—and the less you will earn.

You have become successful because you invested your money in your own best interest.

If you have invested successfully you will:
1.   Have a rather large income
2.   Have a real estate contract collection service to free you of this chore
3.   Have an increasing equity growth
4.   Have an understanding of contracts

With this you can move on to another form of investing for which you have been trained.

In Chapter 6, we talked about the three important factors for someone who wants to buy contracts. These same factors hold true for you now. They are:
1.   Value of property
2.   Yield on your money
3.   Title status of the equity

During the time of your investing you should have learned quite a bit about these three considerations. If you still don't fully comprehend them, don't despair. They will be explained in greater detail in this chapter.

AN 8-CYLINDER APPROACH

You should take caution in trading your money for these longer-term commitments. Let's review these three consider-ations and then point out a few more.
1.   Make sure there is plenty of value above your loan. The lower the excess equity, the less you should be paying for a contract. For example, if you are buying the equity between a $50,000 receivable and a $40,000 payable and the house is worth $52,000, you are running a fine line. But if the value of that house is $70,000, then there is plenty of protection as a buffer. In short, you want the people who are making pay-ments to you to have a lot to lose, as an incentive for them to keep their payments current.

2. Yields—It's important to get your money back as quickly as possible. Watch for high yields, but also remember:
   a. Buy contracts that are likely to cash out quickly, such as on a house qualifying for all types of financing later. (Typical investment properties have a higher probability of staying intact and not cashing out earlier than the final pay off date. Good residential property will sell many times.)
   b. Take a broad view of the whole equity structure. Sometimes properties with excellent equity protection might have a slightly lower yield.
   c. Watch your repay percent. Shoot for a one percent repay of the contract equity. If it's higher, great, but be cautious if it goes below that. You might be able to get it for a lower price, but in case you need to sell, it may be difficult.
3. Make sure you're buying what you bargained for—that your seller has no encumbrances against him, or that he hasn't encumbered this equity. You are buying his exact position, so make sure you know what it is. Get title insurance.
4. Confirm that you have the right to resell your contract. Buy contracts that others will also want to buy in case you have to sell to get some cash.
5. If you don't like bookkeeping, find an effective contract collection service to handle your accounts.
6. Be on the lookout for good deals all the time. Let it be known through the paper or at real estate offices that you're in the market. Be choosy. Take the ones that fit your needs.
7. Determine the location where you want your contracts to be. The two opposing viewpoints are these:
   a. I want my contracts in several states in case one area is hit with hard times.
   b. I want them all right here in this city in case of problems. (I tend to agree with "b," as control is important.)

8.   Avoid contracts with all kinds of entanglements. There cannot be a gamble. Make sure there are definite time periods and some sort of penalties if the conditions of the contract are not met.

These are a few of the things to consider. There are many subjective factors that only you can put a value on. In a nutshell, the price to pay is what you are willing to give.

In order to see what can be done for retirement, let's look at a set of contracts that would be a comfortable retirement for the average person. This represents two and a half years of work at two houses a month.

60 Contracts x $11,000 Average Equity = $660,000 Total Equity

The following is the asset and liability breakdown:

$1,080,000 Assets
   -420,000 Liabilities
   $660,000 Total Net Worth

$105 Average Monthly Payment
   x 60 Contracts
$6,300 Total Net Monthly Income

If you could live on $2,000 a month, what could you do with the excess $4,300? Consider:

1.   These payments come in for many years but are not indefinite.
2.   Long before the incoming payments stop, the underlying loans are paid off; your total net monthly income increases each time one gets paid off.
3.   You are paying a relatively small amount of taxes each year on the installment method. You claim and deduct interest payments.

Since you have made the decision to slow down and start buying contracts, now comes the exciting part. I've found that investing $4,000 to $5,000 a month in contracts takes about 3-5 hours a month. This time includes:

1. Placing an ad to buy contracts or using other ways of notifying people of your intentions
2. Negotiating the deal after you have:
    a. Obtained the title report
    b. Looked at the property
    c. Checked all other factors
3. Closing the transaction

Once you have tried this method, you will see how trouble-free buying contracts is. Following the steps above, you can take your $4,300 and buy a $7,500 contract with a $75 monthly payment.

Now, let's see what you have done to enhance your overall situation:

1. You still have the previous equity (and it's probably even a little larger now).
2. You have added $75 a month to your income so next month you'll have $4,375 to do it again.
4. In terms of inflation, if your living requirements go up by 10 percent to $2,200 by the next year and you have purchased 12 contracts, you will have added around $900 (12 X $75) to your net monthly income. This is much more than the $200 increase you need. (Since you will be purchasing increasingly larger contracts, it will probably be even higher.)
5. Some of these larger contracts can be purchased by saving for a few months.
6. Taxes are handled on the installment sales method. For example, let's say you buy a $10,000 contract for $6,000. Your profit will be $4,000. Divide that by the $10,000 and your installment profit ratio is 40 percent. Therefore, 40 percent of every principal payment needs to be claimed as you receive it. If the

payment is $100, of which an average of $30 is principal—totaling $360 for the year—you will have to claim 40 percent of that or $144. (Remember interest income is treated as ordinary income.)

7.   You have added to your net worth, another asset that is easy to handle and fully protected, as well as producing more monthly income.

CONSOLIDATING YOUR POSITION

One of the most exciting aspects of reaching this level of excess income is the chance to operate from a position of strength. To keep moving forward—building your net worth and net monthly income—there are two ways to go. One is to go out and find other people's contracts, which we covered earlier. The second, and probably the most logical way, is to buy the contracts which are your underlying payments.

Notice that I didn't say pay them off, but buy them at a discount. In our previous example we ended up with $1,080,000 in assets and $420,000 in liabilities. These liabilities represent many people who would like to get at some cash. Wouldn't it be exciting if you could back that liability figure down to zero? Already the debt-to-asset ratio is excellent, but how much better would you feel if it were $320,000 or $220,000—and eventually zero?

Buying these underlying loans should be handled just like the others. Put out the word that you will pay people off, and eventually they will start selling—not always at first, but when they need cash they will know where to come. If someone has an $8,000 contract equity that you are making payments on, and they will take your $4,300 cash for it, how much better off would you be then? Many of the benefits are the same as in the previous example, but a few are different:

1.   You've changed your debt to asset ratio for the better.
2.   You've eliminated another payment, saving you time.
3.   You may have gotten closer to the first mortgage

position, and possibly may be able to assume their underlying loan at a lower interest rate.

In that you have 60 contracts, you probably have 80-90 underlying mortgages. You should look at them and make offers on the best ones. What is best in this case?
1. The ones with higher interest rates.
2. The ones with higher payments in relation to the mortgage amount.
3. The ones with excess restrictive clauses.

If you follow this course, within two years you will have liabilities down to $220,000, and your net monthly payments will have grown from the $6,300 to $8,200.

Buy up all the inside contracts you can, but keep your eyes open for outside contracts also. You probably won't be able to purchase all of your payables at discounted rates. Some contracts won't be discounted. Banks seldom discount them to individuals even when it is in their best interests to do so. You should take an 8-cylinder approach to this concept.

CONCLUSION

All that I wanted in an investment plan came to fruition with this new approach. The ease of this retirement aspect makes it all worthwhile. You will be able to enhance your position with very little effort. So put it on automatic pilot and stay by the controls. Your money machine is intact and running smoothly. Now it's time to go fishing.

Owner Financing

A CONVERSATION WITH WADE COOK

The following question and answer conversation was carried on between myself and a skeptical radio personality not too long ago. I thought it good to put it in this booklet format because it also answers many questions about the Money Machine concept that have been raised around the country. I am convinced you will find the information useful when you are dealing with people who want cash for their equity instead of monthly payments.

Q. **What exactly is meant by a contract or a contract sale?**

A. A contract for sale of real property is an agreement stipulating the conditions under which you will sell your property. Lately it has taken on a general meaning of owner financing, meaning that the owner, instead of the bank, finances all or part of the owner's equity.
The documents used could be a real estate contract or any of its cousins: a mortgage, or in some states, a deed of trust. But no matter which document is used, the gist is that the seller is carrying the financing, and he will earn the interest payments, not the bank.

Q.   **What other names may be found for transactions like that?**

A.   We might refer to it as a contract sale. It might also be called a wrap-around mortgage or an all-inclusive trust deed.

Q.   **Why did you sell on contract so many times?**

A.   Most of the properties I did not sell on contract were in the first years of my investing. At that time I was continually faced with having to sell properties and when problems arose concerning taxes or when other problems occurred dealing with banks, I just naturally took the easier course, and what I consider to be the best course, which is to sell on contract.

To further answer your question, because I was willing to sell on contract, I was able to choose among many, many different buyers, who only had to live up to my standards and my qualifications, rather than the banks'. As I mentioned before, I was faced many times with selling my houses and I found that selling on contract was the fastest way to move them. I wanted to get some money back either on the down payments or on promises to receive money down the road, and to keep my investment plan turning.

I can empathize now with the home sellers who ask themselves whether or not they should sell on contract, because I was faced with that question so many times.

Q.   **Isn't the bookkeeping of selling on contract a big pain?**

A.   Not really. There are principal and interest payments coming in on the payments received. If it's a balloon payment, all you have to do is let the interest accrue and figure out what it's going to be at the end of the time. There are some questions concerning the taxes, yet, once the formula is understood, it is not that hard to compute. Let me explain further. When you're selling on contract you'll be able to take advantage of claiming your profits as you receive them.

There is a simple ratio for figuring that out. All that is involved, basically, is taking the profit that you make on a piece of property, dividing it by the selling price, and coming up with a ratio. Now, you're going to apply that ratio to each and every principal payment as you receive it. That would include the down payments which go toward principal pay-off. You will be able to claim those profits as you receive them. Once that initial bookkeeping is done, another advantage comes through the ability to pay those taxes with inflated dollars.

Q. **Do you have to claim it for tax purposes in that manner?**

A. Not necessarily. If you want to claim the whole sum this year, you may elect to do so. You do not have to claim on the installment sales method. Though I highly suggest that a person who is selling on installment sales should claim according to this method. Very few real estate properties are ever foreclosed on compared to the huge number of properties that are bought and sold every day. If a foreclosure ever did occur and you had already claimed the profits, you would have to back up and do a nice "song and dance" routine to get your money back. If you claim the profits as you receive them and you foreclose, then you take the profits you have received so far, and end it there. Now you have the property back, and it is probably worth more.

Q. **What about tax on the interest collected? Do I still have to claim that when selling on contract?**

A. Yes. If you have payments coming in, you will have to claim the interest as ordinary income. That's the beautiful cost of making a profit.

Q. **Is there any limit to how many properties I can sell on contract at one time?**

A. No. Not only is there no limit to how many different

properties you can buy and sell on contract, there is no limit to how many times the same piece of property can be bought and sold on contract. For instance, you might buy and sell it from somebody on contract, turn around and sell it a year later to somebody else on contract. State laws vary, so if you're doing a lot of these, check to see what the requirements are.

Q. **Does the contract itself have any value other than just collecting money every month? Can it generate any other kind of income?**

A. Yes. Let's go to an example. Let's say, for instance, that we wanted to avoid taxes and we sell a property on an installment sale. We earn $10,000, but spread it out over the whole length of the time we receive it. Also, let's say that we take nothing for a down payment and we just have a $10,000 contract with $100 a month coming in. Suddenly our situation changes. We need a little bit of cash. We can take that equity contract down to get a loan, which is borrowed money, and we pay no taxes on that money.

So our contract can be used effectively for collateral purposes. Be sure, though, to keep the ownership of the contract in your name. If it is going to be pledged as a security, it should say, "The assignment of this contract is given for collateral purposes only." Also, if you're getting a loan from the bank and the bank wants to receive the payments from the contract, have the money deposited into your savings account and then drawn out to make the loan payment.

Whatever you do, make sure that all the wording stays in your name and that there is no real assignment to the bank. If there is an assignment to the bank, the IRS might deem it a sale and make you claim your profits at that time.

Q. **What are the reasons for selling using this method?**

A. If a person selling a piece of property thinks that he can make a fair profit, the tax advantages of the installment sales method (being able to claim profits as received) is incentive enough. Let me give you an example: Suppose a property has a high negative cash flow, meaning that a person has a property and the rents coming in are less than the payments going out. If he can sell that same piece of property and receive higher monthly payments from somebody else buying it from him, then it would be in his best interest to sell the property, alleviate the negative cash flow (which can be a real burden,) get a down payment and some kind of monthly payments coming in so that he can take the money and reinvest it in still other properties.

It does not even have to have a negative cash flow. Some people may be tired of rental headaches and would rather have a steady monthly income, letting someone else worry about collecting rents. Other times, people may be moving and can't worry about the problems. A nice check in the mailbox once a month is no worry at all.

Q. **What kind of equity contracts are there?**

A. An equity contract refers to the amount of money that is now owing the seller or lien holder. For instance, where the owner sold the property, he has two options for creating an equity contract. He can either let somebody else assume his existing loans and pay him his equity on contract, or he may carry the whole balance of the loan. This method leaves the underlying loans intact. The seller stays responsible for them and makes the payments on these underlying loans.

Q. **What are some of the advantages of each way? Obviously, a person can do either.**

A. Okay, let's talk about the final one, where the seller lets the buyer assume his loans. The advantage of this way is that he no longer is responsible for making monthly payments on the existing loans and liens. This can alleviate quite a hassle for some people. All the seller is going to do is receive monthly payments. For example, let's assume his equity is $20,000. He and the buyer agree on $200 a month. He will have that amount to spend with no other obligations. The advantages of the second way are two-fold. The seller is going to maintain a little bit more control. Now, he's going to have to ask himself if this control is worth it. He is going to keep the underlying loan. He knows the underlying payment is going to be made because he is the one making it. The buyer is going to be making a $600 a month payment on the underlying loan (if those are the payments).

He then will have his $200, but it will represent the difference between the $800 payment and the $600 payment. The other point is this: When he sells on a wrap-around contract, he is not only going to be earning interest on the $20,000, he will be earning interest on the unpaid balance of the $80,000 loan. Let's say the underlying interest rate is 10%. He will only get a 2% spread on the $20,000. But he will be getting the full interest on the $80,000 loan. So there is a difference in interest amounts.

Q. **Let's say I have a house. I've sold it on contract, I have some people making payments for three years, and all of a sudden — no payments. The people disappear. What do I do? What are my options?**

A. Both the buyer and the seller are protected under the terms of the contract. If the buyer does not make the payments, or does not live up to the obligations of the contract, it would be an easy foreclosure to divest the buyer of his rights to the property. If they've disappeared and they're not making the payments anymore, it is a simple process to get the property back. Now you would have the property back and would be able to sell it at hopefully a higher price, because of inflation and other improvements. One might think that the buyer might run down the house, but in all my contracts this was very seldom the case. Usually the buyer, because he's buying and not just renting, comes in and fixes up the house. I've only had one bad experience where the buyer was starting to fix up the house; he had in fact ripped out several walls in a major attempt to remodel and made the house less attractive than it was before. He died and left the house in a bad state. His wife couldn't fix it and I ended up getting the house back in a worse condition than it was when I sold it. But in all the other houses sold on contract, the buyers improved the houses by putting on additions, fixing up the interior and exteriors, and taking care of the yards.

If you do need to enforce your rights, it's a simple matter of contacting an attorney and starting the process. This legal expense will have to be paid by your buyer before he can reinstate the loan with you. Your rights are very strongly worded in the estate contract or deed of trust.

If you foreclose on a seller, you will need to work with a very good attorney so you can understand the state laws in regards to the buyers' rights; namely, whether you need to return any money to him or refund any equity that he has built up. In most states where you foreclose, you get the house back "as is, where is." The house becomes yours once again. You are free to sell it or dispose of it in any way you please.

Q. **Is there anything in particular that I can do at the onset of the contract that will help insure the payments will keep coming in?**

A. Well, the payments are basically stated in the contract. There's nothing more that you would want to add to that. The wording is there and it is worded in the seller's favor. If there are other terms that you are agreeing to, yes, you would want to make sure that they are in precise language, stated right in the contract that both of you sign. This will make sure that there is no misunderstanding of the obligations that both of you need to perform.

Q. What about insurance? Someone is buying my house on contract. Do I maintain insurance or is that their obligation?

A. That is their obligation. Likewise, it will state in one of the paragraphs of the real estate contract that the buyer will get insurance, at least enough to cover the loan balance owing you, but usually he'll get insurance to cover the fair market value of the house. You don't need to carry insurance.

You would be listed as the loss payee, or the policy will have a contract of sale document. You and any other people who have a lien against the property would also be listed on the insurance policy. Now, if the buyer ever allows his policy to lapse or even gets close to it, you will also receive notice and will be able to take precautions at that time to protect yourself and your interests.

Q. What have you found are the best methods for advertising properties for sale?

A. When an owner is willing to sell a house on contract and is willing to do so with very flexible terms, meaning that he is able to take a low down payment or no down payment and carry the contract, the best way to get to the largest number of buyers so he can pick and choose from among the best, is to advertise through the newspaper. I also know that I enjoy selling my properties to other investors. I know that investors are coming in to use the properties as rental units or possibly to fix them up further and resell them. I know they're looking for a place to make improvements, not just a place to hang their hat; they want a place to improve, to build some equity of their own. For this reason, I always look for investors.

Q. I've heard of people selling their contracts. Is that a possibility?

A. Yes. There are a lot of people out there who think very highly of real estate contracts. What are you going to get for your contract? Obviously, if these investors are going to be taking their money down the road and they're going to be giving you cash today, they want to give you a discounted amount.

Now, I know a lot of people who do just that. They buy a property, fix it up, and sell it on contract because they can sell it so quickly, and then they turn right around, discount the contract and sell it. I would suggest, as stated earlier, if you need cash, one of the first things you should do is get a loan using your contract as collateral, because you'll pay no taxes.

What they are willing to pay for the contract depends on what they consider important. Some people look at the interest rates you are charging. Some people look at the monthly payments or any balloon payments to see how fast their money will come back in. Some of them look at the equity position of the contract. If it's at the top end, or the middle, they put different values on it.

When it comes right down to it, what you're going to get for your contract is what somebody is willing to pay for it. But you can enhance that amount by shopping. If I had a contract for sale, and I've sold a lot of my contracts, I would call four or five people and say, "Here are the figures. Here's the address. What would you give me for this?" And then I just take the highest bidder.

Q. What about balloon payments?

A. If you need cash at some future time and it is agreeable to the buyer, then maybe some kind of arrangement for larger-than-normal payments, due at some future day, may be in line. But I don't like them.

Once in a while I agreed to them when I was purchasing property, but in every case they turned out to be real headaches. I told myself that I would never make anybody promise to pay me one, and I got along splendidly without them. There are too many things that can get out of control which can place real hardships on people. I just wanted the steady monthly payments.

Q. **What interest rates would I charge if selling on contract? Should I charge what the banks are charging?**

A. Let's look at the main housing problem that exists in America today. When interest rates are high, smaller banks are forced to pay such high amounts for their money that they must loan out their money at even higher rates. These interest rates disqualify buyers — they can't afford the high monthly payments. It used to be that if you bought a house for $120,000 the payments were going to be between $950 and $1000. Now if you buy a house for $120,000, the payments are going to be between $1,000 and $1,200.

Not many people who want to live in a house this size can even qualify for the loan. So, what the banks have done is price themselves right out to the market. I know savings and loans and banks all over the country right now that are not even making loans. They tell their customers that they don't feel justified in charging higher rates, and maybe that's true, but they don't have the money to loan at these high rates and they're having a hard time qualifying people. I talked to one loan officer who said that he had talked to 15 people for an average-sized house and only one qualified. So they shut down their loan officer's desk, realizing they were just wasting their time.

Now, if you as a seller want to find yourself in the same position of not having any buyers who can afford the house or make the payments, then go ahead and charge the high interest rates. But, if you would like somebody to come in and buy your property, and you are more concerned about having a nice, steady monthly income, then I would suggest that you charge a rate that is fair. Fair is what you and the buyer can negotiate; what is affordable.

I think it is fair to charge what banks are paying on their loans, not what they are charging. For instance, if the banks are paying 8% to 10% for savings accounts and they're charging 12% on their loans, then maybe you ought to look at charging 9%-11%. Then you'll have people who can afford to buy a property, and you'll have a lot of buyers to choose from. When banks are paying 3% and charging 8%, you need to look at charging 7%.

Q. **Once we're ready to sign the papers, is there someone who can help me, the novice, fill out the papers so it's all legal?**

Title companies

A. Yes. Obviously, attorneys are very adept at filling out the forms. <u>Title companies and escrow companies</u> can also fill out the forms. Forms are drawn up, though, in such a simple manner, that it's almost a fill-in-the-blank process. There are books written that literally give the terminology and phraseology that can be used for filling the details. I wrote one myself. *good escrow officer*

I suggest the easiest place to go is to a <u>good escrow officer</u> who can process all the papers. If he can't handle the entire transaction, he can find competent help. You can share with them your fears, the things that you want, and the things negotiated between you and the buyer and the escrow person will include these things in the right places.

Q. **What are the steps I need to follow to sell my property this way?**

A. The following steps are given as a basic guideline. Different properties may require additional footwork, but generally speaking, selling your property will come together properly if you:

Step 1. Do some research on the value of your property. Also, determine what you're willing to take and how you are willing to take it.

Step 2. Sit down with your buyer and negotiate the exact terms. Make suggestions and be open to suggestions. Compromise when necessary. Remember, one-sided deals may fall flat. Make sure everyone benefits.

Step 3. Draw up an earnest money agreement. Don't trust anything to just the spoken word. This agreement will become the foundation for the whole transaction, so fill it out in detail.

Step 4. Deliver the earnest money agreement and any changes or addendums to an escrow company (or whomever you choose to handle the closing) and have him start drawing up the papers.

Step 5. Go about doing anything that you are committed to doing while your buyers do the same.

Step 6. Inspect the papers carefully. Don't assume anything. Make sure they are exactly what you want.

Step 7. Sign the papers and transfer possession of the property.

Q. **Let's say I choose to sell on contract. Can I do it with a Realtor? And if so, does it demand that I ask a bigger down payment?**

Realtor

A. The answer is yes and no. Yes, you may sell your house on contract with a Realtor acting as your agent. In many cases if both the seller and buyer know absolutely nothing about real estate, using a Realtor would be appropriate.

A good real estate agent fills a vital roll for people who do not understand real estate. The good ones are worth every dollar they earn. Because of the lending situation, many of them are becoming the champions of creative and flexible financing. Their innovative solutions have glued together many deals that may have been discarded. Sit with them and explain your needs. Let them come up with the solutions.

Whether or not you have to charge a larger down payment depends on the relationship with the real estate company. If the company is willing to take its commissions on contract with monthly payments, or is willing to take commissions on a note payable at some future time, you would not have to charge more cash as a down payment. If the real estate company absolutely demands cash, then the seller has two choices. He can either pay the real estate company the cash and therefore have to demand more down from his buyer or he can find another real estate company that is willing to be more flexible with their commissions.

Q.   **In reality, do real estate agents ever take their commissions on contract?**

A.   Yes. And the more troubled the real estate market gets, and the fewer number of sales that are made, the more flexible they become. Remember though, they need to eat, too. Look around for a good agent. What they're saying now is, "Hey, I might as well have this money, at 8% interest, a year from now, or whatever, than nothing." So, they're able to squeeze these deals into their normal activities.

Q.   **When selling a house on contract, what about other costs I have incurred? For instance, property taxes and insurance that I have already paid in advance?**

A.   There will actually be a day where the title to the property will transfer and the documents will be recorded. This is the closing date. All of these costs that you mentioned, and other costs, will be pro-rated to this day. For instance, let's say that you made the insurance payment for the month and the date of closing is in the middle of the month. The payment that you have already made will have to be paid to you by the buyer from the day of closing.

If property taxes have been paid for the whole year and you're closing the property on July 1, then there will be a refund to you of half of the property taxes you have already paid. Everything will be prorated. By the way, that's exactly what escrow companies are good at: figuring out to the day who has what coming to them so that there is no discrepancy.

Q.   **Who are the people who should sell their house on contract?**

A.   Why don't we reverse the question and ask who is not going to want to sell his house on contract? We'll answer that first. If a person has already committed money to buy another piece of property, he is going to be very desperate in that he needs some cash out of the property he's selling to buy into something else. Those people are not going to be very flexible. They might have to be flexible on their price just to get the cash. For instance, they might have to sell a $90,000 home for $80,000 just to come up with the cash they need.

But, if a person can control how much money he's going to need for the future property and keep that amount very low, he'll be able to sell his present house and receive less money, allowing him to take his equity on contract with payments coming in.

Now to answer your question. I have seen rich people. I have seen poor people. I have seen young and old sell their houses on contract. I've negotiated deals with people from all walks of life and that's not what's important. Their current status only affects them in terms of how they view their options. A person would have to figure out what he wants for himself—whether he wants the monthly payments coming in, whether he wants cash, or whether he is willing to take a lower price for the house to get cash. It's just a matter of sitting down with people and seeing what they want.

Q.   **Obviously, there are advantages to both the cash-out and getting monthly payments. How does a person know which way to go?**

A.   He needs to ask himself, "What is cashing-out going to do to my tax situation? Do I need the cash? What am I going to do with it? Can I get a high return if I finance this buyer?" Let me tell you a few other things. It's been my experience that when people get cash, somehow, all of a sudden, it seems to disappear. One time I saw a couple get $10,000 out of their home and in just a few months the money was gone. Their plans for investing it, sticking it into this and that went up in smoke in a few short months. They had nothing to show for it.

I had another friend who sold a house for a $15,000 equity contract with $200 a month coming in. Every month that money came in like clockwork. He loved it. His rationale was that it was grocery money. The monthly bills keep coming in and it's nice to have those payments coming in to meet them.

One other thing—and this is more of an intrinsic value to having a steady monthly income coming in. You know, as you look at gold and silver and the stock market right now, you see huge ups and downs. You see them fluctuate even more when a president is shot, or when interest rates go up a couple of points, etc. Let's be quite honest, there have been a few dips in the real estate market in the past century, but the dips have been very mild, and all in all, over the last 1,000 years, the price of real estate has continued to go up with very few set-backs or recessions affecting it.

You're talking about one property that is comparable to another property which in turn is comparable to another property on a daily basis. This house in this neighborhood sold for this much, so this other house will sell for this much. Because of that, there is a great stability that is added and enhances the real estate market.

I know a lot of people who feel better about their lives, about themselves, because they have a steady monthly income coming in on these contracts. Not only retired people, but all kinds of people who know that they have $200, $500 and even $1,000 a month coming in on their contracts secured by real estate. They know that this money is going to be there month after month.

Q. **With your books, your lecturing and your experience, you have a pretty good feel for buying and selling on contract. Let me ask this: Is owner financing just a thing of today or will it be around for awhile?**

A. Let's not answer that in terms of looking at the present and then predicting the future. Let's answer it in terms of the past. Owner financing existed long before bank financing. For years, people have been selling property and receiving payments or some kind of trade items for their property.

Along comes the government and along comes heavy bank financing. The banks can loan money and be protected with FNMA, FHA and VA loans. The whole emphasis in the market for the last 50 years has changed to bank financing. The banks came to control the whole market. They were controlling interest rates. They were controlling who qualified, etc. Now all of a sudden, banks are finding that they are out of control because people can't live up to their standards.

But people haven't changed their minds. They're just looking for other ways to buy a house. Looking down the road, all I can say is that if the interest rates stay high then there's going to be a big demand for owner financing. I think this is creating a new awareness in all of the real estate industry as it deals with real estate agents, brokers, investors, and the average home buyer and seller. They're realizing that bank financing is not the only way. There are other sources of money. There is a necessity out there for people to keep buying and selling houses. If they can't do it one way, they'll back up, take another look, and do it another way. After the mind is expanded, it never goes back to its original dimensions. The American people will continue to develop more and better solutions.

Q. So you're saying that if the interest rates go down it will have little effect on owner financing?

A. Yes, we will still see owner financing, but it will have effects in other ways. Let's give a hypothetical case. I sold a house for $70,000 and charged 14% interest with a monthly payment of $800 per month, my equity in the property being $20,000. When the interest rates dropped down to 8%, the person buying the house realized that he could refinance his $70,000 with somebody else and have a monthly payment of $600 or $700 a month. He then refinanced it and I received my $20,000 as a pay-off. Somebody else now stands in my place and I don't have anything else to do with the property. Let's carry that one step further. One of the things that I liked to do was to sell my house on contract, because I could get that money working again on other houses. I learned at that time that the average American lives in his house 3 to 5 years and then sells it.

Most people still believe that bank financing is the only way, so they're out selling their houses with some sort of bank financing. I would get cashed out. I was told that the average time was 3 to 5 years, but with my houses it happened on an average of every two years. So even though I sold on contract, at some time down the road I got cashed out of all the money that was owed to me.

Q. So in other words, selling on contract now is not going to hurt me in the long-run, whether interest rates go up or down, except in the sense of having the security of payments?

A. Yes, that's true. You need to understand that there is a chance that once you sell your house on contract, the contract may run the whole 20, 25, or 30 years. It happens very seldom but could happen. If the rates come down, there's a chance that the person will sell or refinance the house. The only thing that I have learned in my years of investing that always holds true is that nothing remains constant; everything changes. The circumstances will change and the seller will more than likely be on to other things in a few years.

Q. As a short summary then, why should I sell on contract?

A. Well, the first thing is the fact that it might be your only way of selling. Nobody may be able to qualify for your house at the price you're asking. You're going to find a lot of buyers. You're going to have a nice monthly payment coming in. You're going to be able to pay taxes on your profit as you receive it. The amount owed to you is going to be fully protected and secured by real estate. The amount is going to be under the actual value of the real estate and as the value continues to increase, the value position of your loan is going to be strengthened. So, all in all, you are protected. Your investment is strong and healthy.

We think that it is important to understand all the formulas for selling your house creatively, but it is even more important for you to understand exactly how all of these formulas and ratios apply to your specific property. Therefore, please use the easy-to-fill-out form which follows to see exactly what your property will yield you in terms of your installment sales computation, cash to you, monthly payments or balloon payments. We realize the tax considerations, and therefore this form is designed to answer that problem.

CALCULATIONS FOR YOUR PROPERTY

First Year

1. Selling Price .... $ _____
2. Purchase Cost .... $ _____
3. Improvement Cost .... $ _____
4. Other Costs .... $ _____
5. Total Costs (Basis) (Add lines 2 thru 4) .... $ _____
6. Profit from Sale (Subtract line 5 from line 1) $ _____
7. Installment Sales Ratio .... $ _____
   Line 6 divided by line 1 (Profit Sales Price)=____% or
   ._____
8. Down Payment Received .... $ _____
9. Estimated Monthly Payments to be received (Principle Only) .... $ _____
10. Total (Lines 8 & 9) .... $ _____
11. Installment Sales Income (Line 10) _____ x ._____
    =_____ (Ratio from line 7) THIS IS THE AMOUNT TO CLAIM IF PROPERTY IS HELD FOR LESS THAN ONE YEAR.
    Note: If your property is held for over 365 days, your gain will qualify as a long term capital gain and only 40% of the amount received needs to be claimed.

2nd year

12. Estimated principal payments to be received in the second year... $_____

13. Amount from line 12 _____ x Ratio ._____ (line 7) = $_____

THIS IS THE AMOUNT TO BE CLAIMED IN THE SECOND YEAR. If long term, then multiply this figure by current long term rate.

3rd year, 4th year, etc.

The same calculation carries on from year to year. IRS form 6252 is used for reporting property sold on the installment plan method.

Publisher's Note

The preceding conversation is published in a 20-page brochure by Lighthouse Publishing which sells for $5.95. This is in brochure form for you to use as a handout to help others understand the beauty of taking monthly payments instead of taking their equity in cash. Just think how nice it would be to have people refuse to take cash because of the advantages of taking monthly payments as presented here in this chapter and in the brochure. To order *Owner Financing*, see the Available Materials section at the back of the book. Order now and we'll send a special report (that you can copy and use) on why sellers should take monthly payments. It's a real eye opener.

APPENDIX **B**

Available Materials

The following books have been reviewed by the U.S.A. staff and are suggested as reading and resource material for continuing education to help with your real estate investments. Because new ideas and techniques come along and laws change, we're always updating our catalog.

If you would like a copy of our current catalog, write to: U.S.A. Publishing, 24837 104th Ave. SE, Suite 201, Kent, WA 98031. 206–859–2200.

THE WALL STREET MONEY MACHINE $24.95
by Wade B. Cook

The premier book by the nation's premier financial strategist. Eleven fully-explained formulas to help you make 20 to 40% monthly returns in the stock market, just like Wade does. This book, listed on the New York Times best-seller list, is one of the fastest selling books of all time. It has made thousands of people rich. You can be next.

HOW TO PICK UP FORECLOSURES $18.95
by Wade B. Cook

Do you want to become an expert in real estate? This book will show you how to buy real estate at 60¢ on the dollar or less. You'll get there before the auction with no bank financing—the easy way to millions in real estate. The market for foreclosures is a tremendous place to learn and prosper.

OWNER FINANCING $5.95
by Wade B. Cook

A pamphlet you can give to sellers who hesitate to sell you their property, using the owner financing method. Let this pamphlet convince them for you. Special report, "Why Sellers Should Take Monthly Payments," is included.

LEGAL FORMS $29.95
by Wade B. Cook

Numerous legal forms used in real estate transactions are included. These forms were selected by experienced investors, but are not intended to replace the advice of an attorney.

RECORD KEEPING SYSTEM $29.95
by Wade B. Cook

A complete record system for keeping all information on your properties organized. Keeps track of everything from insurance policies to equity growth. Know exactly where you stand with your investment properties and sleep better at night.

101 WAYS TO BUY REAL ESTATE WITHOUT CASH $20.95
by Wade B. Cook

Wade Cook has followed success with success: **101 Ways to Buy Real Estate Without Cash** fills the gap left by other authors who have given all the ingredients but not the whole recipe. This is the book for the investor who wants innovative and practical methods for buying real estate with little or no money down.

THE INCORPORATION HANDBOOK $34.95
by Wade B. Cook

Incorporation made easier! This handbook tells you who, why, and, most importantly, how to incorporate. Included are samples of the forms you will use when you do incorporate.

REAL ESTATE FOR REAL PEOPLE $22.95
by Wade B. Cook

A comprehensive overview of real estate investing. Wade explains all of the strategies, and gives you twenty reasons why you should start investing in real estate today. Learn how to retire rich.

BRILLIANT DEDUCTIONS $159.95
by Wade B. Cook

Do you want to make the most of the money you earn? Do you want to have solid tax havens and ways to reduce the tax you pay? This manual is for you! Learn how to get rich in spite of the new tax laws. See new tax credits, year-end maneuvers, and methods for transferring and controlling your entities.

THE REAL ESTATE CASH FLOW SYSTEM $1695.00

by Wade B. Cook

This six-volume audio-cassette set, originally sold separately, contains everything you'll ever need to begin investing in real estate immediately, do so successfully, handle all of the business aspects and retire sooner than you ever thought possible. Just look at all the tremendous information that can be yours:

Part 1: MONEY MACHINE ALL DAY SEMINAR VOL. I

Spend eight "jam packed" hours of real estate education with one of the foremost experts in the country today. You'll experience a thorough, easy to understand seminar that can lead you to financial independence, wherever and whenever you're in the mood to listen.

Here's a list:

TAPE 1
- How to build up steady monthly income.
- How to get your assets producing more cash flow.
- Understanding the bottom line key to wealth creation.
- Ingredients for making the deals work.
- Choosing types of loans to assume.

TAPE 2
- How to get the good deals to come to you.
- Questionnaire for prospective buyers.
- The 2 key words for making a lot of money in real estate.
- Selling properties on a wrap.
- How to develop cash flow for 30 years.
- How to make money on every deal.

TAPE 3
- Understanding the three things that can destroy your financial empire.
- Why and where you should incorporate.
- How to set up your corporation to meet your families needs.
- Comprehending the 3–entity approach to investing.

TAPE 4
- How to use chaos to get rich.
- Think big in bite–size pieces.
- How to control without ownership.
- Ownership–Control–Cash Flow: They don't have to be the same.
- How to divide up your assets if you're rich or just starting.

TAPE 5   • Understanding the tax brackets.
- Active and passive investments: how they don't work together.
- How to lower your tax brackets.
- How to protect existing properties.
- "S" or "C"–which is best for you.
- The complete explanation of the incredible asset freeze.

TAPE 6   • How to set up your own self–trusteed retirement account.
- How to do the money machine in your pension trust.
- Understanding the types of plans.
- How to get your pension plan to take on your personality.
- Learn the dynamics of the family limited partnership.
- Massachusetts Business Trusts explained and explored.
- How to avoid probate and save huge amounts of taxes with the Living Trust.

MONEY MACHINE TWO–NUPS VOL. II

Money–The Elusive Frontier. This taped home study course is a voyage of the cash flow enterprise. It explores new ways. It gives new insights. Wade Cook the master cash flow strategist will lead you in a full, all–day seminar, teaching you virtually everything you need to know to make quick retirement a reality.

Here's a list:

TAPE 1   • Why real estate is a popular form of investment.
- 3 benefits of ownership – how to get cash flow, tax write–offs, and growth all at the same time, and with little money.
- How to avoid problems most small investors face – hassling with bankers, renter headaches, burying your cash

TAPE 2   • Playing the numbers game.
- How to make money on every deal.
- How to find assumable loans.
- Cash to asset to cash – the most powerful financial concept in America explained.
- Secrets to getting cash back out of investments.
- Finding properties at sub–wholesale prices.

TAPE 3   • How to get your offers accepted.
- How to get people to take monthly payments for their equity.
- Negotiating strategies for beginners.
- The five components of negotiating good deals.
- Closing costs – your key to getting offers accepted.

TAPE 4   • How to get real estate agents to work for you.
- Getting agents to take notes for their commissions and not cash.
- How to enhance the value of the property.
- How to use zero coupon bonds.

TAPE 5   • How to sell fast and at the right price.
          • How to save huge amounts of money on title insurance.
          • How to double your income in future years with no more work.
          • Supercharged ways to process multiple properties.
          • The only way to make the rental game work.
          • How to build an incredible asset base and spread out the tax consequences over 30 years – the installment sale update.
          • How to fill out IRS form 6252.

TAPE 6   • How to quit acting like an employee and start acting like a business owner.
          • Helpful hints – business cards, mobile phones.
          • Entities to use – family limited partnerships, corporations.
          • The problems with joint tenancy.
          • Introduction to living trust.

START SMART REAL ESTATE INVESTING

This cassette tape package will lead you to all the "good deals" you will ever want. As you listen you will be able to go from finding these good deals to actually writing them. This package contains 6 cassette tapes plus a workbook manual.

Here's a list:

TAPE 1   • The secret of leveraging money–only real estate buys and pays for its self.
          • How to avoid 3 problems that stop people from making a lot of money.
          • Instructions on the steps leading up to the Money Machine.

TAPE 2   • The type of assumable loans to look for.
          • How to assume low interest rate loans.
          • The ABC offer method.
          • How to structure each property to produce monthly income.

TAPE 3   • How to get more deals coming your way than you can handle.
          • Properties have problems, people have problems–how to operate so everybody wins.
          • Real estate agents can make you rich.
          • Effective advertising techniques.
          • Other "little known ways" to find super bargains.

TAPE 4   • How to determine value in a property.
          • How to determine the marketability of a property.
          • How to only find properties that can resell quickly.
          • Make sure all terms and conditions of buying are conducive to selling.
          • Low cost fix–up techniques to enhance the selling price.

TAPE 5   • How to bargain for a position of strength.
          • Know what you want before you start negotiating.

- How to choose a good team of professionals.
- How to keep offers simple and powerful.
- How to make sure that the deal holds together.
- Effective use of the property analysis sheets to get the best terms possible.

TAPE 6
- An explanation of the key components of an offer.
- A full explanation of the term, "and or assigns."
- How to fill out the forms as individuals, corporations, or partnerships.
- Using the legal documents to answer questions.
- Proper terminology and how to deal with the sellers equity.
- How to get immediate possession (if possible).
- An escape clause to get you out of the deal if necessary.

GET THE LOW DOWN ON REAL ESTATE

This all day seminar on the innovative and effective techniques that Wade Cook has collected and used for the last fifteen years to buy real estate with little or no cash. Now you won't have to let the good ones pass you by. Use these methods to build a strong asset–based cash flow portfolio.

Here's a list:

TAPE 1
- How to get 3 benefits of real estate ownership with one purchase.
- How low or nothing down deals let you increase wealth exponentially.
- How to make sure all of your investments are measurable.
- Avoiding the common mistakes.
- How to chose your own style of investing.
- How to find the right properties.

TAPE 2
- How to lower the tension when making offers.
- How to find sellers who want to sell more than you want to buy.
- How to use the multiple offer to tie up super bargain properties.
- One sure way to find properties when no one else knows about them.

TAPE 3
- How to get total owner carry back.
- Understanding assumable loans.
- How to use the exculpatory clause.
- Negative amortization = positive capital appreciation.
- Phrases to make the deal work for you.
- How to cut title insurance costs.

TAPE 4
- How to come up with kickers to sweeten the deal.
- How to make ridiculous offers.
- How to use other things rather than cash for down payments.
- How to postpone making your payments.

TAPE 5   • How to raise money if you're dead broke.
         • How to get the seller cash – but not your cash.
         • Information on Title 1 FHA home improvement loans.
         • How to get the seller to get a new loan that you can assume.

TAPE 6   • Government programs that work.
         • How to shift collateral.
         • How to use bonds to buy real estate.
         • Effective techniques to get agents to take monthly payments rather
           than cash.

TAPE 7   • The money machine process as a nothing down technique.
         • How to get an "infinite" return on your money.
         • How to use each property as a springboard for the next property.
         • How to create more cash flow than you can spend.

TAPE 8   • How to use existing rents for your down payment.
         • How to assume liens to avoid putting in a lot of cash.
         • Understanding subordination.
         • How to get going and start making offers.

PRE–FORECLOSURE SYSTEM – GET IT BEFORE THE AUCTION

At last, a complete approach to foreclosures. This system gives you a personal seminar for a fraction of the seminar cost and the chance to repeat the course free of charge. You can take notes in the workbook and learn at your own pace. Because there is so much money to be made in foreclosures, Mr. Cook has put the processing forms in the back of this workbook. Section 2 is blank forms that you can copy and use for your own deals. Section 3 is forms that are filled in so you can see a property from start to finish.

Here's a list:

TAPE 1   • How to find properties before the bank takes them back.
         • Alternatives to REOs.
         • Determining if there are redemption rights.
         • How to find properties way below market value.
         • How to help the seller save his/her credit by making up their back
           payments.

TAPE 2   • How to find properties in early states of foreclosure process.
         • A full explanation of the time line.
         • Cure date, sale date, notice of default and notice of trustee sale
           explained in detail.
         • How to save money when buying the property.

TAPE 3 • Where to find, and how to read foreclosure legal notices.
        • The components of trustee sale notice that will help you process only the great deals.
        • Using attorneys and real estate agents to get you to the deals before everyone else.
        • Other efficient methods for finding these distress methods.

TAPE 4 • How to make sure the property is truly a bargain.
        • How to get information out of the attorney (trustee).
        • How to save money on the closing costs.
        • How to make sure the existing loan is assumable and workable.
        • Doing your homework – making sure you understand the proper chain of title.

TAPE 5 • How to find the home owner.
        • Make sure the proper people sign the documents.
        • Make sure the deed is properly signed.
        • How to get everything ready for quick processing.
        • How to make sure, in finishing the process, that all of your i's are dotted and t's crossed.
        • The 4 steps to finish the process.

TAPE 6 • What to do with the property now that you own it.
        • Deducting the expense of purchasing – things your CPA does not know.
        • Make sure that by purchasing wholesale you're able to make a lot of money on each transaction.

PAPER TIGERS

This is Wade Cook's exciting new tape set on the buying, selling and using of deep discounted mortgages. This seminar will get you up and going in this incredibly profitable business. This complete system will get you started from scratch. If long term, hassle free income is what you are looking for, look no further.

Here's a list:

TAPE 1 • The note buying business – why you should get involved in 2nd mortgages.
        • The 4 ways of making money in the note buying business.
        • Explanations of straight carry backs and wraps.
        • How to build up your monthly income in case something happens to your existing job or business.
        • The 4 reasons why notes on houses are best.

TAPE 2 • The 7 ways to find super discounted mortgages.
        • How to effectively use the court house – hint, don't go after the new listings.
        • Using real estate agents.

• How to get 40% plus yields on your money.
• How to compensate for wrong information.

TAPE 3
• How to do your homework quickly and efficiently.
• How to use the different questionnaires in the workbook to determine equity, yields, and offering prices.
• How to think through and make sure each purchase fits your financial situation.
• Know your exit on each deal.

TAPE 4
• How to find notes and make them better.
• Restructuring for unparalleled growth.
• How to double your money every 7 weeks.
• How to increase the yields on existing deeds of trust.

TAPE 5
• How to attract investors to this business.
• Simple joint ventures made easy.
• How to use a small corporation to buy right.
• How to create a tax problem (we will solve the problem in other sessions.)
• 10 reasons why people should invest their money in your notes.

TAPE 6
• Structuring your business.
• How to use the family corporation in conjunction with your other legal entities.
• The Pension Plan – a perfect vehicle for purchasing notes.

The appendix includes sample ads, letters, legal agreements and questionnaires.

HIGH PERFORMANCE BUSINESS STRATEGIES $159.00
by Wade B. Cook

Your business cannot succeed without you. This course will help YOU become successful so your company can succeed. It is a combination of two previous courses, formerly entitled: "Turbo-Charge Your Business" and "High-Octane Business Strategies." For years Wade Cook and his staff have listened to people's questions, and concerns. Knowing problems are solved by people who know the ropes, Wade's staff wanted to do something more. They categorized the questions and came up with about 60 major areas of concern. Wade then went into the studio and dealt head on with these questions. It's a comprehensive collection of knowledge to get you started quickly.

Here's a list:

Tape 1
- Corporate arrangements – getting the family involved.
- Using corporations to make sure your family gets everything.
- How to have multiple entities so everything is taxed at 15%.
- How to get complete liability protection.
- Using the corporation to control your assets.
- How the officers and directors avoid liability.
- How to have and use different classes of stock.

Tape 2
- Nevada reasoning
- Paper trails
- Needed licenses
- Part of the puzzle
- Reducing taxes
- S or C – which is best?
- Corporate pension planning
- Making more – keeping more
- Bookkeeping techniques
- Bombproofing the business

Tape 3
- You – sine qua non to success
- Your highest and best use
- Special methods of achievement
- Effective management techniques
- Finding the proper fit
- Options for the boss
- Seeing the whole picture
- Priorities – not goals
- Leverage people
- Leadership – new ways

Tape 4
- Getting more sales
- Big results from limited budget
- Enhance everything you do
- Innovative advertising ideas
- Workable ways to "Get Famous"
- Bring order out of chaos
- Closing strategies
- Presentations, etc.
- Monitoring for sure results
- Negotiate for more money

Tape 5
- Choosing business entities
- Determine control methods
- Year ends and more
- Establishing workable solutions
- Saving money
- Tax aspects
- Analyzing structures
- Realize bigger profits
- Fitting it together
- Faster asset accumulation

Tape 6
- Make it an "us" company
- You get what you inspect
- Innovation for the ranks
- Confirmation from the top
- Support the troops
- See the whole picture
- Encourage failure
- Choosing a "star"
- Getting your "A" team
- Brainstorming ideas
- Excel your growth

WEALTH 101/UNLIMITED WEALTH $159.00
by Wade B. Cook

Wealth 101 "University of Money Making Ideas" home study course helps you improve your money's personality. The heart and soul of this seminar is this: make more, pay fewer taxes, keep more for your retirement and family.

Here's a list:

TAPE 1	• Enhance your asset base, leverage, cash flow, and income producing strategies. • Bring quality to your investments.
TAPE 2	• Proper blends of cash flow, tax strategies and appreciation. • Get your investments to work as hard as you do.
TAPE 3	• Active and passive ways to beef up your wealth potential. • Using the benefits to grow faster.
TAPE 4	• Using the different forms and entities. • Learn the real key to protecting your growth.
TAPE 5	• Insights into the "Three Entities." • A full scale dedicated approach to controlling your financial destiny.
TAPE 6	• Learn the three reasons for proper planning: to provide for the continuity of your assets.

THE FINANCIAL FORTRESS $1695.00
by Wade B. Cook

This eight-part set is the last word in entity structuring. It goes far beyond mere financial planning or estate planning, and helps you structure your business and your affairs so that you can avoid the majority of taxes, retire rich, escape lawsuits, bequeath your assets to your heirs without government interference, in short–bomb-proof your entire estate. There are six audio cassette seminars on tape, an entity structuring video and a full documents kit. Look at the following sampling of what is in this set:

PENSION POWER

The word "empower" is overworked today, but in regard to your own great retirement that is exactly what this course will do for you–literally put the power in your own hands to control your financial destiny. You'll discover the ins and outs of money control. You'll see this "power–full" entity come alive. You'll be in the drivers' seat– a seat in a machine that will maneuver well in the fast track.

You'll be in the drivers' seat– a seat in a machine that will maneuver well in the fast track.

Here's a list:

TAPE 1 • Setting up a "safe harbor" for your money.
         • How to set up a self-trusteed pension plan.
         • How to immediately start saving on taxes.
         • Choosing the right plan for you.
         • How to avoid excessive fees charged by the big guys.

TAPE 2 • An explanation of the two major types of pension plans.
         • How to put aside up to $30,000 per year.
         • Determine which business organization to use.
         • How to combine the types of plans for maximum growth.

TAPE 3 • How to act like the big guys with your small business.
         • How to roll over money from existing plans.
         • Step–by–step process in setting up your plan.
         • Everything you wanted to know about vesting.

TAPE 4 • How to wear the different hats.
         • How to get the pension money to take on your personality.
         • What you can and cannot invest in.
         • How to aggressively get your money compounding at over 20% a year.

TAPE 5 • How to set up a "tax free entity."
         • How to go from Chevrolet to Rolls Royce in less than two years.
         • How to avoid capital gains taxes.
         • How to set up a plan to keep your money totally safe.
         • How to stay in control of your financial destiny.

TAPE 6 *(This is an interview by Wade Cook with one of America's foremost pension administrators.)*
         • Understanding the relationship with the plan sponsor, administrator, and trustee.
         • How to set up and operate a "self trusted" pension plan.
         • How to make your money grow faster than you ever thought possible.
         • How to avoid all the common mistakes.
         • How to get really rich and get ready for a great retirement.

THE LIVING LOVING TRUST

Living Trusts are a very important part of your financial puzzle. Every adult needs one, no matter how rich they are. For living, for death, they are an indispensable component of your overall financial situation. A living trust is far reaching and has a dynamism all its own. But it is not a stand-alone entity. This Living Trust Seminar explores and exposes all.

Here's a list:

TAPE 1
- How to chose the right vehicle to get to your financial destination.
- How to avoid probate, provide for the continuity of your assets and eliminate or reduce estate taxes.
- An explanation of 3 kinds of estates.
- The trust relationship explained.
- How to avoid the horrible problems of probate.
- An explanation of what a living trust does and does not do.
- The remarkable QTIP provision.
- How to make sure that everything is established in a tender, loving caring way.

TAPE 2
- How to make sure all the proper players are in place.
- How to provide for your children and/or grandchildren.
- How to use the durable power of attorney.
- The pour over will explained.
- How your living trust will control your other assets.
- How to keep it updated.

TAPE 3
- The problems with joint tenancy explained.
- How to use different forms of ownership.
- A complete explanation of the stepped up basis.
- How to become worth millions, but have your taxable estate near zero.

TAPE 4
- Complete explanation of the entities available.
- How to use an irrevocable life insurance trust.
- How to use Internal Revenue code 351 for transferring assets to corporation.
- A diagram of how to set up your family's business affairs.

TAPES 5 AND 6
- These are the same exact tapes! The information on these first four cassettes is so popular that many people have asked for information to share with family members. We have included two bonus tapes with this course, entitled "A Living Trust Overview." These are about 45 minutes in length and are easy listening for those who need to have a good basic understanding of what the living trust is all about. A brief one-page outline is given in the back of the workbook. Our recommendation is to listen to this tape with whomever you want to learn this information.

FINANCIAL SAVVY

Each of these tape sets is necessary for understanding the different pieces of the puzzle. Financial Savvy is the "capstone" of Wade's career. It puts it all together. It shows you how to fit your own assets, entities, companies, family desires and needs into a workable plan that will be a joy while you're alive, and out–live you for decades.

Here's a list:

TAPE 1
- How to make yourself invisible.
- How to split up your assets.
- How a corporation fits into your financial picture.
- Tax reasons for moving properties into a corporation.

TAPE 2
- How to use more than one entity for making money.
- When to use an "S" corporation.
- An explanation of the 80% exclusion rule.
- How to deduct $17,000 every year for equipment.

TAPE 3
- 3 stages of wealth accumulation.
- How to stay in control of your money.
- How to avoid debt.
- Rolling stock explained.
- How to use zero coupon bonds.
- Know your exit before you go in the entrance.
- How to avoid costly entanglements.
- The ultimate investment – your own gray matter.

TAPE 4
- Understanding what financial planning is all about.
- How to chose a good financial planner.
- Understanding money management.
- The 7 keys to wealth–building today.

TAPE 5
- The choices of business entities.
- Why you should avoid being the sole proprietor.
- Why a corporation is a great estate planning tool.
- The power of Nevada corporations.

TAPE 6
- How to fill out proper legal forms.
- How to integrate the different entities.
- How to set up your partnership.
- How to use the "dispute resolution" agreement to avoid lawsuits.
- Understanding the documents available to you.

AMAZING MONEY MULTIPLIER TECHNIQUES
Dozens of techniques for making more and keeping it.

OFFSHORE TAX HAVENS
Highly advanced strategies for accumulating wealth and passing it along without huge tax bites. Includes a discussion of I.B.C.'s and the four-step method.

taxes.

ENTITY INTEGRATION VIDEO

Structure your affairs completely, and put all the entities together in a fully protective, wealth-enhancing system.

THE WALL STREET WORKSHOP VIDEO SERIES $1995.00
by Wade B. Cook

Eleven albums, sixteen hours of intense instruction in rolling stock, options on stock split companies, writing covered calls and eight other tested strategies designed to help you earn 18% per <u>month</u> on your investments. Filmed live at a Wall Street Workshop, Wade Cook is at his dynamic best. By learning, reviewing and implementing the strategies taught here you will gain the knowledge and the confidence to take control of your investments, and double their value every 2 1/2 to 4 months. Best of all, it will be all in cash, protecting you from any downturn in the market, and giving you an income you can live on. There is no other video in existence that can give you this information, or that can extend the possibility to you of becoming a millionaire in just three years.

Here's a list:
ALBUM 1   • Getting Started
ALBUM 2   • Writing Covered Calls
ALBUM 3   • Rolling Stock/Rolling Options
ALBUM 4   • Options/Proxy Investing
ALBUM 5   • Money Multipliers
ALBUM 6   • Early Bird Session
ALBUM 7   • Stock Market Dynamics
ALBUM 8   • Short Sales/Hedges
ALBUM 9   • Inosculation of Strategies
ALBUM 10   • Entity Structuring
BONUS BINDER   • Two workbooks to help you work through everything

ZERO TO ZILLIONS $995.00
by Wade B. Cook

A four album, 16 cassette, powerful, audio workshop on Wall Street – understanding it, playing it successfully, and retiring rich. Learn powerful investment strategies, eleven of them, as you drive. Learn to avoid pitfalls and losses. Learn to catch "day-trippers" and how to "bottom fish." Learn to write covered calls, and to double your money in one week on options on stock split companies. Wade "Meter Drop" Cook can teach you how he makes 300% per year in his accounts. You then will have the information to try to follow suit. Each album comes with a workbook, and the entire workshop includes a free, bonus video, called "Dynamic Dollars," 90 minutes of instruction in how all the strategies integrate, and giving actual examples of what kinds of returns are possible, so you can get in there and play the market successfully. A must for every savvy, would-be investor.

Here's a list:
ALBUM 1 • The Millionaire Mindset
ALBUM 2 • Writing Covered Calls
ALBUM 3 • Enhanced Returns/Minimized Taxes
ALBUM 4 • Exponential Returns

SPECIAL OFFER

U.S.A. has put these home study courses together in the most comprehensive format ever designed. Investing in the whole package could save you close to ONE THOUSAND DOLLARS!

CALL FOR DETAILS AND TO FIND OUT WHEN MR. COOK WILL BE IN YOUR AREA.

1–800–872–7411

About Wade Cook

Mr. Cook started investing during the late 70's in the Pacific Northwest. He successfully developed an exciting system that created wealth coupled with growth, cash flow with large tax write–offs, and added in a pinch of excitement that has motivated investors everywhere to keep going.

He currently lives in Kent, Washington with his wife, four daughters, and son. From there he travels the country extensively, teaching his unique investment concepts.

Wade authored his first best-selling book "How To Build A Real Estate Money Machine," in 1981 and since then has written and published 14 other books on investing. His books and investor aides are hailed by beginning and experienced investors alike as easy to read and functional reference material. The backbone of these concepts has been distilled from the knowledge he gained by actually doing what he teaches. He is truly America's Premier Financial Strategist.

A WORD ABOUT COOK UNIVERSITY:

As you try to live the American Dream, in the life-style you want, we stand by ready to assist you. People enroll in COOK UNIVERSITY for a variety of reasons. Usually they are a little discontented with where they are– their job is not working, their business is not producing the kind of income they want, or they definitely see that they need more income to prepare for a better retirement.

The backbone of the one-year program is the Money Machine concept–as applied to your business, to stock investments, or to real estate. Although there are many, many other forms of investing in real estate, there are really only three that work: The Money Machine Concept, buying second mortgages, and lease options. And of these three, the Money Machine stands head and shoulders above the rest as a way of accumulating wealth very aggressively. The REAL ESTATE CASH FLOW BOOT CAMP is a three-day course designed to get your Money Machine well-launched. It is one of three major seminars within Cook University. The second is the WEALTH ACADEMY a business enhancement through asset structuring, reducing taxes, and planning and preparing for the future seminar. The third seminar is our famous Wall Street Workshop.

It is difficult to explain COOK UNIVERSITY in only a few words. It is so unique, innovative and creative that it literally stands alone. The Wealth Academy has no equal. But, what would you expect from someone like WADE COOK? Something common and ordinary?

The quality and quantity of the information is virtually unheard of in this country. The Wealth Academy is setting new standards in financial education - leaving all others lagging far behind. The backbone of these concepts is the Money Machine - Enhancing your asset base with assets that produce monthly income allowing you to live the lifestyle you want to live.

We are embarking on an unprecedented voyage and want you to come along. If you choose to make this important decision in your life, you'll also be invited to share your successes in a book Wade is writing called, **Blueprints for Success.** Yes, it takes commitment. Yes, it takes drive. Add to this the help you'll receive by our hand-trained experts and you will enhance your asset base and increase your bottom line.

We want to encourage a lot of people to get in the program right away. You could save you thousands of dollars, if you don't delay. Call right away! Class sizes at WEALTH ACADEMY are limited so each student gets personal attention.

Perpetual monthly income is waiting. We'll tell you how to achieve it. We'll show you how to make it. We'll watch over you while you're making it happen. Thank you for your consideration. We hope to see you in the program right away.

COOK UNIVERSITY is designed to be an integral part of your educational life. May we encourage you to call and find out more about this life–changing program. The number is 1–800–872–7411. Ask for an enrollment director.

TRAVEL AGENT INFORMATION KIT

Have we got some exciting news for you! Because of Mr. Cook's extensive travel, he became a travel agent. Now, this is not like a full scale agent—he's an outside agent. Any reader of this book can be an outside travel agent with a full-service travel agency, but without all the hassles (computers, office space, employees). You'll save lots of money on hotels, car rentals, "FAM" (Familiarization) Packages, etc. If you are going on one big trip, or two smaller trips this year, it's worth it. This is not a travel club. You'll be a travel agent and the perks of being one will be available to you. Use for business or pleasure and if you choose you may also make a lot of money. U.S.A. has put together a Travel Information Kit. This kit includes cassette seminars, brochures, related information - everything you need to make a decision. (Price includes shipping and handling - $15.00.)